Czech

PHRASE BOOK

Zuzana Zrůstová

Consultant:
Daniel Freeland

BBC Books

BBC Books publishes a range of products in the following languages:

ARABIC	GREEK	POLISH
CHINESE	HINDI URDU	RUSSIAN
CZECH	ITALIAN	SPANISH
FRENCH	JAPANESE	THAI
GERMAN	PORTUGUESE	TURKISH

For a catalogue please contact:
BBC Books,
Book Service by Post,   Tel: 01624 675137
PO Box 29,   Fax: 01624 670923
Douglas,
Isle of Man,
IM99 1BQ

BBC books are available at all good bookshops or direct from the
publishers as above.

Developed by BBC Languages

Project Management: Stenton Associates

Design: Steve Pitcher

Published by BBC Books
A division of BBC Worldwide Ltd
Woodlands, 80 Wood Lane, London W12 0TT

ISBN 0563 40041 2

First published 1996

© Zuzana Zrůstová 1996

*Text and cover printed in Great Britain by
Clays Ltd, St Ives Plc*

2

Contents

How to use this book

▌ This book is divided into sections for different situations, such as Road travel, Shopping, Health and so on. Each section contains:

- Useful tips and information
- Words and phrases that you'll see on signs or in print
- Phrases you are likely to want to say
- Things that people may say to you

▌ In the GENERAL CONVERSATION section you will find all-purpose phrases. Some are 'ready-made' phrases which can be used instantly, and there are questions like 'Do you have ...?', to which you can add one of the words listed in the Dictionary at the back of the book.

▌ You can use phrases from other sections in the same way. Many of them can be adapted by substituting another word from the Dictionary. For instance, take the question **Je to daleko na letiště?** (Is it far to the airport?). **Je to** means 'Is it', **daleko** means 'far' and **na letiště** means 'to the airport'. If you want to know if the *station* is far away, just substitute **nádraží** (the station) for **letiště** to give **Je to daleko na nádraží?**

▌ All the phrases are listed with a simple pronunciation guide based on English sounds. The transcription system used is explained in PRONUNCIATION, which might well be the best section to start with.

▌ You will notice that there are sometimes two forms of verbs used in the phrases: this is because Czech has slightly different verb endings (in the past tense), depending on whether the speaker is male or female, and whether it's a woman or a man being spoken to or referred to. We have tried to reduce the number of these phrases to a minimum to avoid confusion.

▌ If you want some guidance on how the Czech language works, see BASIC GRAMMAR, page 12.

■ The ENGLISH-CZECH DICTIONARY starting on page 140 contains both expressions used in the phrases for easy reference and words which may expand your vocabulary.

■ And finally a few handy tips:

■ Wherever possible, work out in advance what you want to say: if you're going shopping, for instance, write out a shopping list in Czech. If you're buying travel tickets, make a note saying where and when you want to go, how many tickets you want, single or return, etc. It is useful to remember a few key words for every situation which can help you get your meaning across.

■ Don't try to come out with long, grammatically correct sentences. Keep it simple. You can convey a lot with just a few words (and gestures).

■ Do not worry too much about the grammar. Even if you do not get the endings right, people will understand what you are saying if you use the right words.

■ Practise saying things out loud. This will help you get used to some unusual or difficult sounds.

■ If you fail to explain what you want to say or ask, try to find the word or phrase in the book and show it.

■ When listening to what other people say, try to concentrate your attention on some key words which may help you understand what you need to know. You will get an idea of what these key words may be from expressions listed under the heading **You may hear** included in each section.

■ Don't be shy. The Czechs do know that their language is difficult and all your attempts to speak it will be appreciated as a gesture of goodwill rather than a necessity.

■ And finally, a practical request: the Czech Republic and its people are undergoing unprecedented changes. While this book has been compiled with care and to the best of our knowledge, some information may become obsolete or irrelevant. We welcome any suggestions and comments about this book.

■ In the meantime, have a good trip – **šťastnou cestu!**

The Czech alphabet

■ Several letters of the Czech alphabet use a diacritical mark ˇ which denotes different (softer) pronunciation. The letters **q**, **x**, and **w** are found only in names and words of foreign origin. The combination of the letters **c** and **h** represents one sound (**kh**).

You may hear

Jak se to píše?   *yak* se to *pee*she   How is it spelt?

Letter	Pronunciation	Letter	Pronunciation
a	aa	ň	eny
b	bai	o	aw
c	tsai	p	pai
č	chai	q	kvai
d	dai	r	er
ď	dyai	ř	erzh
e	ai	s	es
f	ef	š	esh
g	gai	t	tai
h	haa	ť	tyai
ch	khaa	u	oo
i	ee	v	vai
j	yai	w	dvoyitai vai
k	kaa	x	iks
l	el	y	ipsilon
m	em	z	zet
n	en	ž	zhet

Pronunciation

▌ Czech spelling is phonetic. This means that each letter (with the exception of **ch** which is considered as one letter) denotes one sound (what you see is what you hear). Once you know how to pronounce the individual letters of the alphabet, you will be able to read Czech words with relative ease.

▌ You do not have to master perfect pronunciation to make yourself understood. For the purely practical purposes of this book pronunciation is simplified.

▌ The sign ˇ over a letter signifies a new sound and the sign ´ lengthens the pronunciation of vowels.

Stress

▌ In Czech, stress always falls on the first syllable. Stress or its absence do not change the quality – pronunciation and length – of a vowel. For example the final **a** in **voda** is pronounced in the same way as the **a** in **ano** (not like the 'a' in the English 'sofa'), and even unstressed vowels can be long (the **á** in **káva** and in **černá** are equally long). In phrases and sentences the main stress is marked in bold in this book.

Vowels

▌ Each of the five short vowels found in Czech has a long counterpart marked with an acute accent [´]: **a** – **á**, **e** – **é**, **i** – **í**, **y** – **ý**, **o** – **ó** or with a little circle over **u**: **u** – **ú/ů** .

▌ The vowel **ě** is pronounced either like 'ye' in 'yes' (**bě** – bye, **pě** – pye, **vě** – vye) or with the tongue pressed even closer against the

8

palate, rather like in 'cognac' (**ně** – nye, **tě** – tye, **dě** – dye, **mě** – mnye).

i/í and **y/ý** have identical pronunciation.

There is one diphthong (combination of two vowels pronounced as one syllable) in Czech, namely **ou**. Other combinations of vowels (**au**, **eu**, **ea**, etc.) mostly represent two syllables (thus **mu-ze-um**, for example, consists of three syllables).

E at the end of words is always pronounced (as the English 'e' in 'ten', but never like the 'e' in 'he').

	Approximate English equivalent	Shown in book as	Example	Pronounced as
a	a in 'cat' (northern English) or u in 'but' (southern English)	a	**tak**	tak
á	a in 'father'	aa	**pár**	paar
e	e in 'ten'	e	**den**	den
é	ai in 'pair'	ai	**lék**	laik
ě	ye in 'yet'	ye	**věk**	vyek
i/ y	i in 'pin'	i	**list / typ**	list / tip
í/ý	ee in 'cheese'	ee	**pít / sýr**	peet / seer
o	o in 'hot'	o	**stop**	stop
ó	as in 'awe'	aw	**milión**	miliawn
u	u in 'put'	u	**suk**	suk
ú/ů	oo in 'soon'	oo	**úl / sůl**	ool / sool
ou	o in 'no'	oh	**soud**	soht

Consonants

Most consonants are pronounced in a similar way to English.

Consonants are sometimes found in groups of up to five (**čtvrt** – chtvrt), which may be difficult for an English person to pronounce (inserting a vowel can help: chtvert).

Consonants **b**, **d**, **g**, **h**, **v/w**, **z**, and **ž** are sometimes pronounced **p**, **t**, **k**, **ch**, **f**, **s**, and **š** at the end of syllables and words.

The sign ˇ over a consonant denotes a different sound (e.g. **s**, pronounced as the same letter in English, when written **š** becomes 'sh' as in the English 'shot').

The Czech **r** is rolled, rather like Scottish.

ř is perhaps the most difficult sound to learn. It can be imitated with a combination of rolled **r** and the sound **zh** (as 's' in 'leisure').

1. The following consonants are pronounced almost as in English:

	Aproximate English equivalent	Shown in book as	Example	Pronounced as
b	b in 'but'	b	**banka**	banka
p	p in 'cup'	p	**pas**	pas
d	d in 'day'	d	**den**	den
t	t in 'cut'	t	**typ**	tip
f	f in 'fit'	f	**filtr**	filtr
g	g in 'gas'	g	**golf**	golf
h	h in 'hit'	h	**hit**	hit
k	ck in 'kick'	k	**kam**	kam
l	l in 'luck'	l	**les**	les
m	m in 'my'	m	**my**	mi
n	n in 'no'	n	**ne**	ne
p	p in 'cup'	p	**pan**	pan
s	s in 'sock'	s	**sen**	sen

t	t in 'hot'	t	**tam**	tam
z	z in 'zone'	z	**zub**	zup
v	v in 'van'	v	**ven**	ven

2. The following consonants are pronounced differently in Czech (**q** and **w** are only found in words of foreign origin):

c	ts in 'fits'	ts	**moc**	mots
ch	in 'loch'	kh	**chróm**	khrawm
j	y in 'yes'	y	**jak**	yak
q	k + v in 'cook vegetables'	kv	**Aqua**	akva
r	r (rolled)	r	**rok**	rok
w	v in 'van'	v	**Werner**	verner

3. The following consonants with a little sign over them are pronounced differently from their unmarked equivalents:

č	ch in 'chin'	ch	**čin**	chin
ď	d in 'duet'	dy	**ďábel**	dyaabel
ň	gn in 'cognac'	ny	**koňak**	konyak
ř	r in 'try'	rzh	**tři**	trzhi
š	sh in 'shot'	sh	**šest**	shest
ť	t in 'tune'	ty	**ťukat**	tyukat
ž	s in 'leisure'	zh	**žert**	zhert

Note: **d, t, n** followed by **i** and **ě** have the same pronunciation as **ď, ť, ň** : **dítě** (dyeetye), **tisíc** (tyiseets), **nikdo** (nyigdo).

Basic grammar

■ Czech, which is spoken by some ten million people, belongs to the western branch of Slavonic languages, together with Polish, Serbian and Slovak. These languages are characterised by inflexion, that is a complex system of word endings conveying different meanings. Thus a large part of Czech vocabulary (nouns, adjectives, pronouns, verbs and numerals) is made up of words which have several different forms depending on their role in a sentence.

Nouns

Gender

■ Unlike English (but like many other European languages), all Czech nouns have a grammatical gender: masculine (*m*), feminine (*f*) or neuter (*n*). With the exception of some nouns (**chlapec** – boy, **královna** – queen, **dítě** – child), the grammatical gender is not related to the meaning and has to be looked up in the dictionary. However, some clues may help determine the gender:

■ Most masculine nouns end in consonants: **pes** (dog), **dům** (house), **pokoj** (room). A small group of masculine nouns end in **-a**, and **-e**.

■ Most feminine nouns end in the vowels **-a** (**dívka** – girl) or **-e** (**židle** – chair). Smaller groups of feminine nouns end in consonants (e.g. **mrkev** – carrot, **věc** – thing). Feminine first names almost always end in **-a** (**Jana**, **Kateřina**) and the typical feminine ending in surnames is **-ová** (**Nováková**) and sometimes **-á** (**Černá**).

■ Neuter nouns only end in vowels. All nouns ending in **-o** (**město** – town) are neuter. Other neuter endings are **-e/-ě** (**pole** – field, **kotě** – kitten), and **-í** (**nádraží** – railway station).

Plural endings

Most masculine and feminine nouns end in -i/-y or -e. Neuter nouns end in -a and -í, less frequently in -e. There are no simple rules to form plurals, but a few clues will help at least in some cases:

Masculine gender

– the overwhelming majority of masculine nouns referring to human beings end in -i: **muži** (men).

– the ending -y is reserved for masculine inanimate nouns: **obchody** (shops).

Feminine gender

– all nouns ending in -a form the plural with -y: **dívka** – **dívky** (a girl – girls), **opera** – **opery** (opera – operas).

– all nouns ending in -e retain this ending in the plural: **židle** – **židle** (a chair – chairs).

Neuter gender

– all neuters ending in -o form the plural with the ending -a: **město** – **města** (a town – towns).

– all neuters ending in -í retain this ending in the plural: **nádraží** – **nádraží** (a railway station – railway stations).

The gender of a noun affects the form of other words in a sentence (adjectives, verbs) which relate to it. Masculine nouns are further divided into animate nouns which designate living things, and inanimate nouns which designate non-living things. This distinction is also reflected in different endings.

Declension

Noun endings change according to what function the noun has in a sentence. There are seven different cases in Czech, both for singular and plural. (Examples of noun declension are listed under **Adjectives**. However, they do not represent all the existing declension models.)

The **nominative** (the 'dictionary' form) is used to express the subject of the sentence; a person or thing performing the action. It is also found in combination with the verb 'to be':

Matka píše dopis	**Mother** is writing a letter
Jsem *učitel*	I'm **a teacher**
To je můj *syn*	This is my **son**

The **accusative** denotes the direct object of the sentence:

Matka píše *dopis* přítelkyni	Mother is writing **a letter** to a friend

The **dative** designates the indirect object of the sentence, i.e. a person or a thing to whom/which something happens:

Matka píše dopis *přítelkyni*	Mother is writing a letter **to a friend**

The **genitive** is often translated in English with the help of 'of' or ''s'. It is a possessive case designating a person or an object to whom/which something/somebody belongs or refers. It is used with words describing quantity ('a cup of ...', 'a piece of ...') and numerals from five upwards:

přítel mé *dcery*	my **daughter's** friend
šálek *čaje*	a cup **of tea**
pět *hodin*	five **hours**

The **instrumental** designates how/by what means or by whom/with whom something is done:

Poslala dopis *poštou*	She sent the letter **by mail**
Dopis byl napsán *rukou*	The letter was written **by hand**
Šla *se psem* procházku	She went for a walk **with her dog**

The **locative** (prepositional) is only used with certain prepositions (mainly **o** – about, **na** – on, **v** – in):

Píše o *dětech*	She is writing about **the children**
Dopis ležel na *stole*	The letter lay **on the table**
V *případě* nehody volejte policii	**In the event** of an accident call the police

The **vocative** is used to address a person:

Milý *Václave*, ...	Dear **Václav**, ...
Pane!	**Sir!**

Articles

Czech does not use articles (the, a, an) in front of nouns. The meaning of an article is conveyed by other grammatical means and by the context. Thus the word **město** means 'a town' or 'the town', depending on the context:

Jdu do *divadla.*	I am going to **the theatre**.
Našel jsem *peněženku.*	I found **a purse**.

Adjectives

Adjectives (**starý** – old, **cizí** – foreign) agree in number and gender with the noun they are describing. The larger group of adjectives has the nominative singular endings of **-ý** (*m*), **-á** (*f*), and **-é** (*n*). Adjectives ending in **-í** for all genders singular and plural form a smaller group. In the plural, adjectives end mostly in **-é** (masculine inanimate, feminine) and **-á** (neuter). However, adjectives describing animate masculine nouns (*mladí* **muži** – young men, *vzácní* **ptáci** – rare birds) have the plural ending **-í**. Here is the declension pattern for the more common group of adjectives, listed in combination with nouns:

Singular	masculine inanimate	masculine animate	feminine	neuter
nominative	velký dům	malý chlapec	hezká žena	české město
accusative	velký dům	malého chlapce	hezkou ženu	české město
dative	velkému domu	malému chlapci	hezké ženě	českému městu
genitive	velkého domu	malého chlapce	hezké ženy	českého města
instrumental	velkým domem	malým chlapcem	hezkou ženou	českým městem
locative	velkém domě	malém chlapci	hezké ženě	českém městě
vocative		malý chlapče!	hezká ženo!	

Plural

nominative	velké domy	malí chlapci	hezké ženy	česká města
accusative	velké domy	malé chlapce	hezké ženy	česká města
dative	velkým domům	malým chlapcům	hezkým ženám	českým městům
genitive	velkých domů	malých chlapců	hezkých žen	českých měst
instrumental	velkými domy	malými chlapci	hezkými ženami	českými městy
locative	velkých domech	malých chlapcích	hezkých ženách	českých městech
vocative		malí chlapci!	hezké ženy!	

Note: Colloquial Czech uses different sets of endings, for example **malej** instead of **malý**, **hezkejch** instead of **hezkých** etc.

Other words declined like adjectives

Ordinals (**první, druhý** – the first, the second, etc.), possessives (**můj, tvůj** – my, your, etc.) and some question pronouns (**který** – which, **jaký** – what ... like) agree with the nouns in gender and number and follow the same declension pattern as adjectives.

Examples:

druhý den (*m*) (the second day), **druhá řada** (*f*) (the second row), **druhé kolo** (*n*) (the second round), **který autobus** (which bus), **jaký je ten film?** (what is the film like?), **k tvému dopisu** (to your letter).

Personal pronouns (I, you, he, she, etc.)

	I	you	he	she	it	we	you	they (*m, f, n*)
nominative	já	ty	on	ona	ono	my	vy	oni/ ony/ ona
accusative	mě	tě/tebe	jeho/ho	ji	je/ho	nás	vás	je

dative	mně/mi	ti/tobě	jemu/mu	jí	jemu/mu	nám	vám	jim
genitive	mě	tě/tebe	jeho/ho	jí	jeho/ho	nás	vás	jich
instrumental	mnou	tebou	jím	jí	jím	námi	vámi	jimi
locative	mně	tobě	něm	ní	něm	nás	vás	nich

Tebe and **tobě** are used after prepositions and under emphasis. In all other instances the shorter forms are used.

After prepositions all pronouns beginning with **j-** change into a form beginning with **n-**: e.g. **Nezávidím jí** (I don't envy her) but **Vezmu k ní děti** (I'll take the children to her).

Possessive pronouns (my, your, his, their, etc.)

These are generally declined. In a sentence, the possessives agree with the noun to which they relate in number (singular or plural) and in gender (masculine, feminine, or neuter). The following table shows the nominative form of possessives in all three genders, singular and plural, and the masculine animate plural (e.g. **moji chlapci** – my boys).

	singular			plural			
	masc.	fem.	neut.	masc. inanim.	masc. anim.	fem.	neut.
my	můj	moje	moje	moje	moji	moje	moje
your	tvůj	tvoje	tvoje	tvoje	tvoji	tvoje	tvoje
his/its	jeho	jeho	jeho	jeho	jeho	jeho	jeho
her	její	její	její	její	její	její	její
our	náš	naše	naše	naše	naši	naše	naše
your	váš	vaše	vaše	vaše	vaši	vaše	vaše
their	jejich	jejich	jejich	jejich	jejich	jejich	jejich

Examples: **jejich děti** (their children), **váš lístek** (your ticket), **moje otázky** (my questions) etc.

Note: The pronouns **můj** and **tvůj** have alternative forms in some cases which are more formal (e.g. **moje dcera**/**má dcera** – my daughter, **tvoji chlapci/tví chlapci** – your boys, **moje děti/mé děti** – my children).

Demonstrative pronouns (this, that, these, those)

The pronouns **ten** (*m*), **ta** (*f*), **to** (*n*), which are used to point to things, can sometimes be used as substitutes for the English definite article 'the'. Their more emphatic form is **tento/tenhle**, **tato/tahle**, **toto/tohle** 'this', and **tamten**, **tamta**, **tamto** 'that'. The distinction between 'this' and 'that' is not as clear as in English.

Like nouns, these pronouns are subject to declension:

	singular			plural			
	masc.	fem.	neut.	masc. inanim.	masc. anim.	fem.	neut.
nominative	ten	ta	to	ty	ti	ty	ta
accusative	toho	tu	to	ty	ty	ty	ta
dative	tomu	té	tomu	těm	těm	těm	těm
genitive	toho	té	toho	těch	těch	těch	těch
instrumental	tím	tou	tím	těmi	těmi	těmi	těmi
locative	tom	té	tom	těch	těch	těch	těch

Examples:

Neznám tu ženu	I don't know the woman
Podejte mi tamten kufr	Pass me that suitcase
O tomto městě jsem už hodně slyšel	I've heard a lot about this town

Verbs

The basic 'dictionary' form of Czech verbs, or the infinitive, ends in **-t**. Verbs, like nouns, are also subject to inflection, i.e. to changes of the form according to person (I, you, he, etc.), number (singular or plural), tense (present, past and future) and gender (in the past tense only). As the verb ending itself, sometimes in combination with the context, indicates the person who performs the action, the pronoun (**já, ty, on** – I, you, he, etc.) can be omitted in a sentence:

(já) Nevím, kde to je   I don't know where it is

Conjugation

The conjugation of verbs (change of endings according to person and number) follows five different patterns. Here are some typical examples of verbs in the present tense:

	dělat (to do)	**vidět** (to see)	**nést** (to carry)	**začít** (to begin)	**slibovat** (to promise)
já	**dělám**	**vidím**	**nesu**	**začnu**	**slibuju**
ty	**děláš**	**vidíš**	**neseš**	**začneš**	**slibuješ**
on/ona/ono	**dělá**	**vidí**	**nese**	**začne**	**slibuje**
my	**děláme**	**vidíme**	**neseme**	**začneme**	**slibujeme**
vy	**děláte**	**vidíte**	**nesete**	**začnete**	**slibujete**
oni/ony/ona	**dělají**	**vidí**	**nesou**	**začnou**	**slibují**

Most verbs follow one of these conjugation models in the present, even if their infinitive forms are different. For example **platit** (to pay) agrees with **vidět**, **umřít** (to die) with **nést**, **zapomenout** (to forget) with **začít**, **pít** (to drink) with **hrát**. All verbs ending in -**ovat** follow the model **slibovat** and all verbs ending in -**at** the model **dělat**.

Some verbs are classified as irregular:

	mít to have	**chtít** to want	**jíst** to eat	**vědět** to know	**moci** to be able
já	**mám**	**chci**	**jím**	**vím**	**můžu**
ty	**máš**	**chceš**	**jíš**	**víš**	**můžeš**
on/ona/ono	**má**	**chce**	**jí**	**ví**	**může**
my	**máme**	**chceme**	**jíme**	**víme**	**můžeme**
vy	**máte**	**chcete**	**jíte**	**víte**	**můžete**
oni/ony/ona	**mají**	**chtějí**	**jedí**	**vědí**	**můžou**

Tense

There are three tenses: present, past and future. Czech does not make the distinction between 'I do' and 'I am doing', or rather expresses this distinction differently from English (see below). In forming the past and future tenses the verb **být** (to be) is used:

	present	past (m/f/n)	future
já	**jsem**	**byl/byla/bylo jsem**	**budu**
ty	**jsi**	**byl/byla/bylo jsi**	**budeš**
on/ona/ono	**je**	**byl/byla/bylo**	**bude**
my	**jsme**	**byli/byly/byla jsme**	**budeme**
vy	**jste**	**byli/byly/byla jste**	**budete**
oni/ony/ona	**jsou**	**byli/byly/byla**	**budou**

Note: the use of the endings **-i/y** in the past plural depends on the subject. **-y** is used for masculine inanimate and feminine nouns, and **-i** for masculine animate nouns or where the subject is mixed (people, pupils etc.).

To form the past tense of regular verbs, replace the infinitive ending **-t** with **-l**, **-la**, or **-lo** for the masculine, feminine, and neuter genders respectively. With some pronouns, the present form of the word **být** is added:

dělat (to do)

já	**dělal, -a jsem**	my	**dělali, -y jsme**
ty	**dělal, -a jsi**	vy	**dělali, -y jste**
on/ona/ono	**dělal, -a, -o**	oni/ony/ona	**dělali, -y, -a**

The future tense is formed with the help of **být** (to be) in the future tense, to which the infinitive form of the verb is added:

já	**budu dělat**	my	**budeme dělat**
ty	**budeš dělat**	vy	**budete dělat**
on/ona/ono	**bude dělat**	oni/ony/ona	**budou dělat**

However, some verbs form the future tense in a different way. To know which verbs they are, distinction must be made between two types of verbs.

Most Czech verbs appear in two forms: perfective and imperfective, reflecting whether the action designated by the verb is complete, that is, occurs only once, or incomplete, that is, repetitive. In English, this distinction is often made with the help of other means, e.g. the simple and continuous tenses:

Četl knížku	He was reading a book
Přečetl tu knížku za jediný den	He read the book in one day

The perfective verbs express the future tense with their present tense forms. Compare:

to write:	**psát** (imperfective)	**budu psát** (I will be writing)
	napsat (perfective)	**napíšu** (I will write)

Negatives

These are formed by adding the prefix **ne-** at the beginning of a verb: **dělá** (he does) – **nedělá** (he does not), **jeli** (they went) – **nejeli** (they did not go), etc.

In Czech, negative verbs are used with negative words, e.g. **nikdy** (never), **nikdo** (nobody), **nic** (nothing), **žádný** (no), etc., where in English the words 'ever', 'anybody', 'anything' or 'any' would be used. **Nedělá nic** means literally: 'He doesn't do nothing'.

Word order and absence of subject

Since both nouns and verbs indicate, with their endings, person, tense and gender, word order is very flexible and the subject of a sentence can be omitted.

Questions

These can be formed either with question words or by changing the tune of an ordinary statement into a rising tune.

Examples:

Jak se dostanu na letiště?	How can I get to the airport?
Je tu parkoviště	There is a car park here
Je tu parkoviště?	Is there a park car here?

▮ A universal greeting is **Dobrý den** (literally Good day) which can be used throughout the day. **Dobré ráno** (Good morning) and **Dobrý večer** (Good evening) are equivalents of this greeting to be used at the appropriate time of day. However, **Dobré ráno** (Good morning) is only used in the early morning (i.e. till about 9 a.m.). Later than that, **Dobrý den!** is more appropriate.

▮ To say goodbye you use the expression **Na shledanou**, or **Dobrou noc** (Good night) when it is late.

▮ You will often hear people say **Ahoj!** (Hi!/Bye!) which is a greeting as well as a way of saying goodbye. It is much more informal than the English 'Hello' and is only used among friends, young people, family members and with children.

▮ When addressing members of various professions and occupations, always use the words **pane** (Mr) and **paní** (Mrs), e.g. **Pane doktore** (Doctor, ...), **Pane řidiči** (Driver ...), **Pane vrchní** (Head waiter ...).

▮ To attract attention in the street you say simply **Promiňte ...** (Excuse me ...) or **Prosím vás ...** (Please ...), or, if it is a child, **Promiň ... , Prosím tě ...** .

▮ In Czech there are two ways of saying 'you' when addressing one person: the informal **ty** and the formal **vy**. **Vy** is also used when speaking to more than one person (compare the French *vous*). The polite **vy** is to be used in a conversation with a person you don't know or with whom you have a formal relationship. Only when you talk to a child, a young person of your age, or a friend, will you say **ty**, e.g. **Jak se (ty) máš?** (How are you?). In all other instances you use the polite **Jak se (vy) máte? Ty** and **vy** are usually omitted in a sentence (see BASIC GRAMMAR, page 12).

▮ Czech has different forms to indicate sex distinctions, e.g. **Angličan** (an Englishman), **Angličanka** (an Englishwoman). Both forms are given in this book, the male form first. Some forms of verbs add an **-a** if a woman is speaking or is being spoken to/about. For example a man will say **Chtěl bych ...** (I'd like to ...), whereas a woman will say **Chtěla bych ...** . In this book the form to be used is indicated by the words 'male'/'female' in brackets. Similarly, you will say **Dal jste mi ...** (You gave me ...) if you are talking to a man and **Dala jste mi ...** if you are talking to a woman. To help you decide which form to use, the explanation you=male or you=female follows in brackets.

▌ The word **Prosím** (please) has different meanings and can be used in the following different ways:

1. as a polite request: **Dejte mi prosím (vás), ...** (Give me ... , please.)

2. as a reply to the phrase 'Thank you': **Prosím** (You are welcome.)

3. as a question: **Prosím?** (Pardon?)

4. as a reply to an apology: **Prosím** (That's all right. No problem.)

5. to invite a customer to express his wish or place an order: **Prosím!** (How can I help you?/What will you have?)

6. to present the customer with something: **Prosím** (Here you are.)

7. to answer the phone: **Prosím?** (Hello?)

▌ It is considered polite to wish other people at the table **Dobrou chuť** (Enjoy your meal) before you start eating.

▌ Note: **Čechy** is sometimes used as a shorter substitute for **Česká republika** (Czech Republic) but, strictly speaking, it describes only the western part of the republic, Bohemia. The eastern part is called **Morava** (Moravia) and its inhabitants will proudly describe themselves as Moravians rather than Czechs, except perhaps when travelling abroad. These two constituent parts form what in English is sometimes referred to as the Czech lands. There is no widely accepted Czech substitute. You will sometimes hear the expression **Česko** but this seems not to have caught the nation's imagination.

Greetings and leave-taking: attracting attention

Welcome	**Vítejte** (polite or directed at more than one person)/**Vítej** (informal)	*veeteyte/ veetey*
Hello/Hi/Bye (informal)	**Ahoj**	*ahoy*
Good morning (only used early in the morning)	**Dobré ráno/jitro**	*dobrai raano/yitro*
Good morning/afternoon	**Dobrý den**	*dobree den*
Good evening	**Dobrý večer**	*dobree vecher*
How are you?	**Jak se máte?** (formal) **Jak se máš?** (informal)	*yak se maate* *yak se maash*
Fine, thanks	**Dobře, děkuji**	*dobrzhe dyekuyi*
And you?	**A vy?** (formal)/**A ty?** (informal)	*a vi/a ti*
Goodbye/See you soon	**Na shledanou**	*naskhledanoh*
Bye, see you	**Ahoj** (informal)	*ahoy*
Good night	**Dobrou noc**	*dobroh nots*
Excuse me!	**Promiňte** (formal) **Promiň** (informal)	*prominyte* *prominy*

Introductions

My name is ...	**Jmenuji se ...**	*ymenuyi se*
Nice to meet you	**Těší mě**	*tyeshee mye*
This is my wife/daughter	**To je moje manželka/ dcera**	*to ye moye manzhelka/ tsera*
This is my husband/son	**To je můj manžel/syn**	*to ye mooy manzhel/sin*
These are my children	**To jsou moje děti**	*to ysoh moye dyetyi*

Talking about yourself and your family

(See also COUNTRIES AND NATIONALITIES, page 129)

I am English	**Jsem Angličan** (male)/ **Angličanka** (female)	*ysem anglichan/ anglichanka*

I am American	**Jsem Američan** (male)/ **Američanka** (female)	*ysem americhan/ americhanka*
I am Australian	**Jsem Australan** (male)/ **Australanka** (female)	*ysem australan/ australanka*
I'm single	**Jsem svobodný** (male)/ **svobodná** (female)	*ysem svobodnee/ svobodnaa*
I'm married	**Jsem ženatý** (male)/ **vdaná** (female)	*ysem zhenatee/ vdanaa*
I have two/three children	**Mám dvě/tři děti**	*maam dvye/trzhi dyetyi*
I have a son/daughter	**Mám syna/dceru**	*maam sina/tseru*
I live in London	**žiji v Londýně**	*zhiyi vlondeenye*
I'm a student	**Jsem student** (male/ **studentka** (female)	*ysem student/studentka*
I'm a teacher	**jsem učitel** (male)/ **učitelka** (female)	*ysem uchitel/uchitelka*
I'm a secretary	**Jsem sekretářka** (female)	*ysem sekretaarzhka*
I'm an accountant	**Jsem účetní** (for both male and female)	*ysem oochetnyee*
I'm a tourist	**Jsem turista** (male)/ **turistka** (female)	*ysem turista/turistka*
I work in ...	**Pracuji v ...**	*pratsuyi f ...*
... an office/a bank/	**... v kanceláři/v bance/**	*f kantselaarzhi/v bantse/*
a factory/a private firm	**v továrně/v soukromé firmě**	*f tovaarnye/f sohkromai firmnye*
I'm here on holiday (if working)	**Jsem tu na prázdninách na dovolené**	*ysem tu na praazdnyinaakh (student)/na dovolenai*
I'm here on business	**Jsem tu služebně**	*ysem tu sluzhebnye*
I arrived ...	**Přijel** (male)/**Přijela** (female) **jsem ...**	*przhiyel/przhiyela ysem ...*
... yesterday/a week ago/ last Saturday	**včera/před týdnem/ minulou sobotu**	*fchera/przhet teednem/ minuloh sobotu*
I don't speak much Czech	**Nemluvím moc česky**	*nemluveem mots cheski*

Jak se jmenujete?	*yak se ymenuyete*	What's your name?
Odkud jste?	*otkut yste*	Where are you from?
Jak dlouho tu zůstanete?	*yak dloh-ho tu zoostanete*	How long are you staying here?
Jak se vám tu líbí?	*yak se vaam tu leebee*	How do you like it here?

Talking about the Czech Republic and your own country

I like it here very much	**Moc se mi tu líbí**	*mots se mi tu leebee*
I like Prague	**Líbí se mi Praha**	*leebee se mi praha*
The Czech Republic is very beautiful	**Česká republika je velmi krásná**	*cheskaa republika ye velmi kraasnaa*
I know Bohemia well	**Znám dobře Čechy**	*znaam dobrze chekhi*
It's my first visit	**Jsem tu poprvé.**	*ysem tu poprvai*
Are you from here?	**Jste odsud?**	*yste otsut*
Have you been to England?	**Byl** (you =male)/ **Byla** (you= female) **jste v Anglii?**	*bil/bila yste f angliyi*
Did you like England?	**Líbilo se vám v Anglii?**	*leebilo se vaam f angliyi*

Jste v Čechách poprvé?	*yste f chekhaakh poprvai*	Is this your first visit to the Czech Republic?
Kde pracujete?	*gde pratsuyete*	Where do you work?

Likes and dislikes

I like ...	**Rád** (male)/ **Ráda** (female)...	*raat/raada*
... reading/travelling/ swimming	... **čtu/cestuju/ plavu**	*chtu/tsestuyu/plavu*

26

... going to the cinema/to the theatre	... chodím do kina/do divadla	khodyeem do kina/ do dyivadla
I don't like cold weather	Nemám rád (male)/ráda (female) studené počasí	nemaam raat/ raada studenai pochasee
I like this dress/this picture	Líbí se mi tyhle šaty/ tenhle obrázek	leebee se mi tihle shati/ tenhle obraazek

Talking to a child/informal conversation

What is your name?	Jak se jmenuješ?	yak se ymenuyesh
How old are you?	Kolik je ti let?	kolik ye tyi let
Do you have any brothers or sisters?	Máš nějaké sourozence?	maash nyeyakai sohrozentse
Have you been to England?	Byl (you=male)/Byla (you=female) jsi v Anglii?	bil/bila ysi f anglyi
How did you like London?	Jak se ti líbil Londýn?	yak se tyi leebil londeen

Invitations and replies

Would you like a drink?	Dáte si něco k pití?	daate si nyetso k pityee
Would you like to go to the cinema/theatre?	Chtěl (you=male)/Chtěla (you=female) byste jít do kina/divadla?	khtyel/khtyela biste yeet do kina/ dyivadla
Sit down	Posaďte se	posatyte se
Yes, please	Ano, děkuji	ano dyekuyi
No, thank you	Ne, děkuji	ne dyekuyi
I'd love to	Moc rád (male)/ráda (female)	mots raad/ raada
That's very kind of you	To je od vás moc hezké	to ye od vaas mots heskai
Please leave me alone	Prosím vás, nechte mě na pokoji	proseem vaas nekhte mnye na pokoyi

You may hear

Dáte si něco k pití?	*daate si nyetso k pityee*	Would you like something to drink?
Dáte si něco k jídlu?	*daate si nyetso k yeedlu*	Would you like something to eat?

Good wishes and exclamations

Congratulations!	**Gratuluji!**	*gratuluyi*
Happy birthday!	**Všechno nejlepší k narozeninám!**	*fshekhno neylepshee k narozenyinaam*
Best wishes!	**Všechno nejlepší!**	*fshekhno neylepshee*
Happy Christmas/Easter!	**Veselé vánoce/velikonoce!**	*veselai vaanotse/ velikonotse*
Happy holidays (at Christmas or Easter)	**Příjemné svátky!**	*przheeyemnai svaatki*
Good luck!	**Hodně stěstí!**	*hodnye shtyestyee*
Have a good journey!	**Šťastnou cestu!**	*shtyastnoh tsestu*
Have a good holiday	**Hezkou dovolenou!**	*heskoh dovolenoh*
Enjoy your meal!	**Dobrou chuť!**	*dobroh khuty*
Cheers!	**Na zdraví!**	*na zdravee*
What a pity!	**Škoda**	*shkoda*
It's wonderful!	**To je nádherné!**	*to ye naadhernai*
That's great!	**To je skvělé!**	*to ye skvyelai*

Talking about the weather

What a lovely day!	**Krásný den**	*kraasnee den*
What terrible weather!	**Strašné počasí!**	*strashnai pochasee*
It's going to rain	**Bude pršet**	*bude prshet*
It's hot, isn't it?	**To je ale horko, že?**	*to ye ale horko zhe*
It's cold, isn't it?	**To je ale zima, že?**	*to ye ale zima zhe*

▌ British, US and all Western European nationals need only a full passport valid for at least another six months to enter the Czech Republic. The British Visitor's Passport is not valid. New Zealand, Australian and Canadian visitors still need a visa, which can be obtained at Czech embassies and consulates. Visas can also be issued at a limited number of border crossings and at the Prague-Ruzyně airport.

▌ To extend your visa or to stay longer than your visa-free period you have to go to the main foreigners' and passport office in Prague (**Úřadovna cizinecké policie and pasové služby**, see USEFUL ADDRESSES, page 137). Foreigners' police offices are in all regional capitals.

▌ Border controls are straightforward. Information on customs regulations can be obtained at the customs head office (see USEFUL ADDRESSES, page 137).

You may see

Autobusové nádraží	Bus station
Celnice	Customs (office)
Celní kontrola	Customs control
Celní prohlášení	Customs declaration
Informace pro turisty	Tourist information
Kouření zakázáno	No smoking
Nádraží	Railway station
Pasová kontrola	Passport control
Stanoviště taxíků	Taxi rank
Zboží k proclení	Goods to declare

You may want to say

I'm here on holiday	**Jsem tu na dovolené**	*ysem tu na dovolenai*
I'm here on business	**Jsem tu služebně**	*ysem tu sluzhebnye*
I'm here for ...	**Jsem tu na ...**	*ysem tu na*
... a week/two weeks	**... týden/dva týdny**	*teeden/dva teedni*
... a month/six months	**... měsíc/šest měsíců**	*mnyeseets/dva mnyeseetse*
I've got something to declare	**Mám něco k proclení**	*maam nyetso k protslenyee*
I have nothing to declare	**Nemám nic k proclení**	*nemaam nyits k protslenyee*
I have 2 bottles of whisky/ three bottles of wine/ three cartons of cigarettes	**Mám dvě lahve whisky/ tři lahve vína/ tři kartony cigaret**	*maam dvye lahve viski/ trzhi lahve veena/ trzhi kartoni tsigaret*
I have a receipt	**Mám na to paragon**	*maam na to paragon*

You may hear

Váš pas prosím	*vaash pas proseem*	Passport, please
Dokumenty prosím	*dokumenti proseem*	Documents, please
Účel vaší cesty?	*oochel vashee tsesti*	The purpose of your visit?
Jak dlouho se zdržíte v České republice?	*yak dloh-ho se zdrzheete f cheskai republitse*	How long are you staying in the Czech Republic?

Changing money

▌ The Czech unit of currency is the crown or **koruna** (Kč) divided into 100 hellers (**haléř**).

▌ Money can be changed at banks (**banka**), bureaux de change (**směnárna, change**), hotels, travel agencies and airports. Banks charge the lowest commission. Exchange offices with their wide network and long opening hours are probably the most convenient places to change foreign currency, but their commission is usually much higher.

▌ The current exchange rates are usually displayed on the premises of banks and bureaux de change. They are also published in the daily press. Two different rates are normally listed: **Nákup** shows the rate at which Czech crowns are sold for foreign currency, while **prodej** is the rate at which foreign currency is sold for Czech crowns. Have your passport ready when changing money. Most banks and money exchange offices accept credit cards.

▌ Although credit cards (**kreditní/úvěrová karta**) are becoming ever more popular, they are not universally accepted as a means of payment. They are only taken at larger hotels, restaurants, international car hire agencies and tourist-oriented shops in major cities. The most commonly recognised cards are: American Express, VISA, Master Card and Access. Traveller's cheques (**cestovní šeky**) can only be exchanged at banks.

▌ Under no circumstances should you change money in the street: not only is it an offence but you may easily fall prey to fraudsters.

You may see

Banka	Bank
Nákup	The rate at which foreign currency is bought
Otvírací hodiny	Opening hours

Otevřeno	Open	Směnárna/	Bureau de
Pokladna	Cashier's desk	Change	change
Prodej	The rate at which foreign currency is sold	Valuty	Foreign currencies
		Zavřeno	Closed

You may want to say

(See also NUMBERS, page 121)

I'd like to change ...	Chtěl (male)/Chtěla (female) bych si vyměnit ...	khtyel/khtyela bikh si vimnyenyit
... pounds sterling	... anglické libry	... anglitskai libri
... some traveller's cheques	... cestovní šeky	... tsestovnyee sheki
... a Eurocheque	... Eurošek	... euroshek
I'd like to get some cash on my credit card	Chci si vybrat peníze na kreditní kartu	khtsi si vibrat penyeeze na kreditnyee kartu
What's the exchange rate today?	Jaký je dnes kurz?	yakee ye dnes kurs
What's the commission?	Jaký poplatek se platí?	yakee poplatek se platyee
Can you give me some change, please?	Můžete mi dát nějaké drobné prosím?	moozhete mi daat nyeyakai drobnai proseem

You may hear

Kolik si chcete vyměnit?	kolik si khtsete vimyenyit	How much do you want to change?
Váš pas prosím	vaash pas proseem	Your passport, please
Můžete jít k pokladně	moozhete yeet k pokladnye	Please go to the cashier
Tady prosím váš podpis	tadi proseem vaash potpis	Sign here, please

Directions

▌ Tourist information centres and major travel agencies sometimes provide a limited range of town plans and maps. There is a wider selection of guides and maps available in bookshops. For local tours and sights visit one of the local tourist centres.

▌ If you want to ask a passer-by for directions, just say **Promiňte, kde je ...** (Excuse me, where is ...) and name the place you are looking for. All simple requests listed below can be followed by the word **prosím** (please). Have the name as it appears on the town plan or written on a piece of paper handy in case your pronunciation sounds unfamiliar.

▌ If you are looking for a particular address, bear in mind that house numbers come after street names (e.g. **Jindřišská 14**).

▌ It is unusual for drivers to stop for pedestrians at zebra crossings.

▌ When you're being given directions, listen out for the important bits. Try to repeat the information to make sure you have understood correctly. If you can't understand something, ask the person to say it again more slowly, prompting with **Prosím?** (Pardon?) or **Pomaleji prosím** (More slowly, please).

You may see

Galerie	Art gallery	**Nábřeží**	Embankment
Hrad	Castle, fortress	**Palác**	Palace
Katedrála	Cathedral	**Pěší zóna**	Pedestrian zone
Kostel	Church	**Přechod pro chodce**	Pedestrian crossing
Most	Bridge		
Muzeum	Museum	**Radnice**	Town hall
Náměstí	Square	**Tržiště**	Market

Třída	Avenue
Ulice	Street
Zámek	Chateau, castle

You may want to say

Excuse me	**Promiňte**	*prominyte*
Pardon?	**Prosím?**	*proseem*
Repeat that more slowly, please	**Ještě jednou pomaleji prosím**	*yeshtye yednoh pomaleyi proseem*
Slowly	**Pomalu**	*pomalu*
Again	**Znovu**	*znovu*
I'm lost	**Zabloudil** (male)/ **Zabloudila**(female) **jsem**	*zablohdyil/zablohdyila ysem*
Where is ...?	**Kde je ...?**	*gde ye*
Where are ...?	**Kde jsou ... ?**	*gde ysoh*
Where is it?	**Kde to je?**	*gde to ye*
Where is the bank?	**Kde je banka?**	*gde ye banka*
Where are the taxis/toilets?	**Kde jsou taxíky/záchody?**	*gde ysoh takseeki/ zaakhodi*
Is there a ... near here?	**Je tu blízko .... ?**	*ye tu bleesko*
Show me on the map	**Ukažte mi to na mapě**	*ukazhte mi to na mapye*
How do you get to the airport/station?	**Jak se dostanu na letiště/nádraží?**	*yak se dostanu na letyishtye/naadrazhee*
Is this the road to Brno?	**Je tohle silnice do Brna?**	*ye tohle silnyitse do brna*
Is it far?	**Je to daleko?**	*ye to daleko*
Is it near?	**Je to blízko?**	*ye to bleesko*
Which tram goes to the museum?	**Která tramvaj jede k muzeu?**	*kteraa tramvay yede k muzeu*
How many kilometres?	**Kolik je to kilometrů?**	*kolik ye to kilometroo*

How long does it take?	**Jak dlouho to trvá?**	*yak* dlouho *to* trvaa
On foot?	**Pěšky?**	*pyeshki*
By car?	**Autem?**	*autem*

You may hear

Rovně/doprava/doleva	*rovnye/doprava/doleva*	Straight on/Right/Left
První/ druhou ulicí ... vpravo/vlevo	*prvnyee/ druhoh ulitsee fpravo/vlevo*	The first/second turning ... to the right/left
Rovně 50 metrů	*rovnye padesaat metroo*	Straight on for 50 metres
Na konci ulice	*na kontsi ulitse*	At the end of the street
Za křižovatkou	*za krzhizhovatkoh*	Behind the crossroads
Daleko/blízko	*daleko/bleesko*	Far/Near
Půl hodiny pěšky	*pool hodyini pyeshki*	Half an hour on foot
Uvidíte ...	*uvidyeete ...*	You'll see ...
Na rohu/za rohem ...	*na rohu/za rohem*	At the corner/Round the corner ...
Vedle/naproti/před/ za	*vedle/naprotyi/przhet/ za*	Next to/Opposite/In front of/Behind

■ Czech traffic regulations are mostly identical with the rest of continental Europe. Standard road signs are used and you drive on the right. Traffic on the right has priority on roads. Seat belts are compulsory in front seats and children under 12 are not allowed to sit in the front. Foreign driving licences are generally recognised. (For the explanation of some signs which may be unusual for foreign motorists see **Road signs** (opposite).

■ You are obliged to have a certificate of insurance, i.e. 'green card', available from your own country, a nationality sticker on your car and to carry a first-aid kit.

■ Drinking and driving is strictly prohibited. You must not have any alcohol in your blood when driving.

■ There are several categories of roads:

- motorways (**dálnice**). The motorway network is not extensive but new motorways are under construction. The main motorway links Prague with Brno and the Slovak capital Bratislava. You have to pay to use motorways.

- European roads (including motorways) marked with an E and a number in a green square.

- first class roads (**silnice první třídy**) marked with a one- or two-figure number in a blue square.

- second class, or branch roads (**silnice druhé třídy**) marked with a three-figure number in a blue square.

■ Speed limits are: 60 km per hour (37 mph) in towns and villages, 90 km per hour (56 mph) on open roads and 110 km per hour (68 mph) on motorways.

■ Unleaded petrol (95 octane Natural) is so far not universally available outside major cities.

■ Driving in central Prague is not recommended because there is so little parking space. There are only a few underground car parks in the city centre. You can leave your car at a supervised car park near an underground station and use the metro. Fines for illegal parking are severe.

∎ Cars can be hired at the Prague-Ruzyně airport, through the Čedok travel agency, the Pragocar company and a network of agencies throughout the country.

∎ If you have an accident you are required to inform the police. For a breakdown service the numbers to call are 123 or 0123 and 154. For information on motoring contact one of the motoring organisations, e.g. the Automotoklub, or the Central Automotoklub Prague (ÚAMK), tel. 123, which also offers various services for motorists.

You may see

Road signs

Autoopravna	Car repairs
Clo	Customs
Dej přednost jízdě zprava	Priority to the right
Hlavní silnice	Main road (yellow diamond sign – you have right of way)
Jednosměrný provoz	One-way traffic
Konec hlavní silnice	End of the main road (yellow diamond sign with a black line across – you no longer have right of way)
Nebezpečí	Danger
Nebezpečná zatáčka	Dangerous bend
Nebezpečná krajinice	Dangerous verges
Objížďka	Diversion
Pěší zóna	Pedestrian zone
Pozor	Caution

Průjezd zakázán	No through road		
Rozsviť světla	Turn on lights		
Slepá silnice	Cul-de-sac/No through road		
Úsek častých nehod	Accident black spot		
Zákaz stání	No waiting		
Zákaz vjezdu	No entry		
Zákaz zastavení	No stopping		
Změna přednosti v jízdě	Change in the right of way		

Other signs

Centrum	Town/city centre	**Pneuservis**	Tyre repairs
Dálniční křižovatka	Junction	**Pokuta**	Fine
Hlídané parkoviště	Supervised car park	**Pronájem automobilů**	Car hire
Myčka/Mycí linka	Car wash		
Odtahová služba	Tow-away service	**Samoobsluha**	Self-service
Parkovací listek	Parking ticket (one you buy)	**Servis/Díly**	Car repairs and spare parts
Parkoviště uzavřeno	Car park closed	**Silnice uzavřena**	Road closed

---

You may want to say

At the garage/service station

Is there a petrol station here?	**Je tu benzínová pumpa?**	*ye tu benzeenovaa pumpa*
96-octane petrol (4-star)	**Super**	*super*
90-octane petrol (2-star)	**Special**	*spetsiyaal*
Unleaded petrol (95 octane)	**Bezolovnatý benzín**	*bezolovnatee benzeen*
Diesel oil	**Nafta**	*nafta*
... litres of super	**... litrů super**	*... litroo super*
Fill it up, please	**Plnou nádrž**	*plnoh naadrsh*

A can of oil/water, please	Plechovku oleje/Vodu prosím	plekhofku oleye/vodu proseem
Can you check ... ?	Můžete zkontrolovat ...?	moozhete skontrolovat
... the tyres/oil/water	pneumatiky/olej/vodu	pneumatiki/oley/vodu
Can you clean the window?	Můžete mi umýt okno?	moozhete mi umeet okno
Where is the air, please?	Kde máte vzduch?	gde maate vzdukh
How does the car-wash work?	Jak pracuje ta mycí linka?	yak pratsuye ta mitsee linka
Can you show me how it works?	Můžete mi ukázat, jak to funguje?	moozhete mi ukaazat yak to funguye
Where can I have my car washed?	Kde si můžu nechat umýt auto?	gde si moozhu nekhat umeet auto
How much is it?	Kolik to stojí?	kolik to stoyee

Parking

Where can I/we park?	Kde se dá zaparkovat?	gde se daa zaparkovat
Can I/we park here?	Může se tu parkovat?	moozhe se tu parkovat
How long can I/we park here?	Jak dlouho se tu může parkovat?	yak dloh-ho se tu moozhe parkovat
How much is it per hour?	Kolik se platí za hodinu?	kolik se platyee za hodyinu

Hiring a car

(See also DAYS, MONTHS, DATES, page 126)

I'd like to hire a car/small car/medium-sized car/large car, please	Chci si najmout auto/maléauto/střední auto/velké auto prosím	khtsi si naymoht auto/malai auto/strzhednyee auto/velkai auto proseem
An automatic	S automatikou	s automatikoh
For three days/a week/two weeks	Na tři dny/týden/dva týdny	na trzhi dni/teeden/dva teedni
From ... to ...	Od ... do ...	ot ... do ...
From Monday to Friday	Od pondělka do pátku	ot pondyelka do paatku

How much is it?	**Kolik to stojí?**	*kolik to stoyee*
Per day/week?	**Na den/týden?**	*na den/teeden*
Per kilometre?	**Za kilometr?**	*za kilometr*
Is mileage included?	**Jsou v tom najeté kilometry?**	*ysoh ftom uyetai kilometri*
Is petrol included?	**Je v tom i benzín?**	*ye ftom i benzeen*
Is insurance included?	**Je v tom i pojištění?**	*ye ftom i poyishtyenyee*
Comprehensive insurance cover	**Havarijní pojištění**	*havariynee poyishtyenyee*
My husband/son/friend ...	**Můj manžel/syn/přítel ...**	*mooy manzhel/syn/przheetel*
My wife/daughter/ girlfriend ...	**Moje manželka/dcera/ přítelkyně ...**	*moye manzhelka/tsera/ prheetelkinye*
... is driving too	**... také řídí**	*takai rzheedyee*
Can I pay with this credit card?	**Můžu platit touto kreditní kartou?**	*moozhu platit tohto kreditnyee kartoh*
Can I leave the car at the airport?	**Můžu nechat auto na letišti?**	*moozhu nekhat auto na letyishtyi*
How do the controls work?	**Jak pracují kontrolky?**	*yak pratsuee kontrolki*
What kind of petrol does it take?	**Na jaký benzín to jezdí?**	*na yakee benzeen to yezdyee*

Breakdowns and repairs

(See also CAR AND BICYCLE PARTS, page 42)

My car has broken down	**Porouchalo se mi auto**	*porohkhalo se mi auto*
This doesn't work	**Tohle nefunguje**	*tohle nefunguye*
Is there a garage around here?	**Je tu někde autoservis?**	*ye tu nyegde autoservis*
Can you get a mechanic?	**Můžete mi sehnat automechanika?**	*moozhete mi sehnat automekhanika*
Can you tow me to a garage?	**Můžete mě odtáhnout do servisu?**	*moozhete mnye otaahnoht do servisu*

Do you do repairs?	Děláte opravy?	*dyelaate opravi*
I don't know what's wrong	Nevím, v čem to je	*neveem fchem to ye*
I think ...	Myslím , že ...	*misleem zhe*
... it's the clutch	... je to spojka	*ye to spoyka*
... it's the brakes	... jsou to brzdy	*ysoh to brzdi*
The car won't start	Auto nechce nastartovat	*auto nekhte nastartovat*
The battery is flat	Baterie je vybitá	*bateriye ye vibitaa*
The engine is overheating	Motor se přehřívá	*motor se przhehrzeevaa*
It's losing oil/water	Teče olej/voda	*teche oley/voda*
It has a puncture	Je to píchlá pneumatika	*ye to peekhlaa pneumatika*
I don't have any petrol	Nemám benzín	*nemaam benzeen*
I need a ...	Potřebuji ...	*potrzhebuyi ...*
Is it serious?	Je to něco vážného?	*ye to nyetso vaazhnaiho*
Can you repair it (today)?	Můžete to (dnes) opravit?	*moozhete to (dnes) opravit*
When will it be ready?	Kdy to bude hotové?	*kdi to bude hotovai*
How much will it cost?	Kolik to bude stát?	*kolik to bude staat*

You may hear

Petrol

Jaký benzín?	*yakee benzeen*	What kind of petrol?
Kolik?	*kolik*	How much?
Klíče prosím	*kleeche proseem*	Keys, please

Parking

Tady nemůžete parkovat	*tadi nemoozhete parkovat*	You can't park here
Je to zadarmo	*ye to zadarmo*	It's free
Parkoviště je támhle	*parkovishtye ye taamhle*	The car park is over here

Hiring a car

Jaké auto chcete?	*yakai auto khtsete*	What car do you want?
Na jak dlouho?	*na yak dloh-ho*	For how long?
Na kolik dní?	*na kolik dnyee*	For how many days?
Řidičský průkaz prosím	*rzhidyichskee prookaz proseem*	Driving licence, please

Breakdowns and repairs

Co s tím je?	*tso styeem ye*	What's wrong?
Otevřete kapotu prosím	*otevrzhete kapotu proseem*	Open the bonnet, please
Tyhle součástky nemám	*tihle sohchaastki nemaam*	I don't have these parts
Bude to hotové za týden/za tři dny/zítra/ do pátku/	*bude to hotovai za teeden/ za trzhi dni/zeetra/do paatku*	It will be ready in a week's time/in three days/tomorrow/by Friday

Car and bicycle parts

Alternator	**Alternátor**	*alternaator*
Battery	**Baterie**	*bateriye*
Brakes (front/rear)	**Brzdy (přední/zadní)**	*brzdi przhednyee/zadnyee*
Chain	**Řetěz**	*rzhetyes*
Clutch	**Spojka**	*spoyka*
Cooling system	**Chladicí systém**	*khladyitsee sistaim*
Distributor	**Rozdělovač**	*rozdyelovach*
Electrical system	**Elektrické vybavení**	*elektrickai vibavenyee*
Engine	**Motor**	*motor*
Fan belt	**Klínový řemen**	*kleenovee rzhemen*
Frame	**Rám**	*raam*
Fuel pump	**Palivové čerpadlo**	*palivovai cherpadlo*

Gearbox	**Převodovka**	*przhevodofka*
Handbrake	**Ruční brzda**	*ruchnyee brzda*
Handlebars	**Řidítka**	*rzhidyeetka*
Headlights	**Dálková světla**	*daalkovaa svyetla*
Ignition	**Zapalování**	*zapalovaanyee*
Indicator	**Směrovka**	*smnyerofka*
Inner tube	**Duše pneumatiky**	*dushe pneumatiki*
Lights (front/rear)	**Světla (přední/zadní)**	*svyetla przhednyee/zadnyee*
Oil filter	**Olejový filtr**	*oleyovee filtr*
Pedal	**Pedál**	*pedaal*
Pump	**Čerpadlo**	*cherpadlo*
Radiator	**Chladič**	*khladyich*
Radiator hose	**Hadice chladiče**	*hadyitse khladyiche*
Reversing lights	**Zpětná zadní světla**	*spyetnaa zadnyee svyetla*
Saddle	**Sedlo**	*sedlo*
Silencer	**Tlumič**	*tlumich*
Spare wheel	**Rezerva**	*rezerva*
Spark plugs	**Zapalovací svíčky**	*zapalovatsee sveechki*
Spokes	**Paprsky kola**	*paprski kola*
Starter motor	**Motor startéru**	*motor startairu*
Steering	**Sízení**	*rzheezenyee*
Transmission	**Převodovka**	*przhevodofka*
Tyre	**Pneumatika**	*pneumatika*
Tyre pressure	**Tlak v pneumatikách**	*tlak f pneumatikaakh*
Valve	**Ventil**	*ventil*
Wheel (front/rear/ left/right)	**Kolo (přední/zadní/ levé/pravé**	*kolo przhednyee/ zadnyee/leval/pravai*
Windscreen	**Čelní sklo**	*chelnyee sklo*

■ Private taxi services supplement public transport in most towns and cities and are relatively cheap. Taxis are usually marked with a broken black stripe and with the sign **taxi**.

■ There are different rates per kilometre set by law. For example, for rides within the city of Prague, the day rate is **taxa** 1. Night rates are higher. Always check that the meter is set on the correct rate. All taxis have meters which should show the rate per kilometre, any surcharges and the fare for the distance covered. Taxi drivers will expect a 5–10 percent tip.

■ Caution is recommended when taking a taxi in the capital, Prague. The safest bet is to book a taxi in advance by telephone. There are many firms with round-the-clock service; these are listed in the telephone directory.

■ The fare can be negotiated in advance and you can ask for a receipt at the end of the journey before you pay if you suspect that you have been overcharged.

■ Avoid taxis waiting at taxi ranks near busy tourist spots where you run the risk of being overcharged. Flagging down a taxi in less congested areas may be a better alternative.

■ At the Ruzyně airport check at the information counter on the approximate charge for a taxi ride to the city centre.

You may want to say

(See also DIRECTIONS, page 33)

Is there a taxi rank near here?	**Je tu někde stanoviště taxíků?**	*ye tu nyegde stanovishtye takseekoo*
Can you order me a taxi?	**Můžete mi objednat taxi?**	*moozhete mi obyednat taksi*

Immediately	**Hned**	*hnet*
For tomorrow at nine o'clock	**Na zítra na devátou hodinu**	*na zeetra na devaatoh hodyinu*
From ... to	**Z ... do/na ...**	*z ... do/na ...*
To the airport/station	**Na letiště/nádraží**	*na letyishtye/naadrazhee*
From the Forum Hotel	**Z hotelu Forum**	*z hotelu fawrum*
To this address, please	**Na tuto adresu prosím**	*na tuto adresu proseem*
Is it far?	**Je to daleko?**	*ye to daleko*
How much will it cost?	**Kolik to bude stát?**	*kolik to bude staat*
Switch the meter on, please	**Zapněte prosím taxametr**	*zapnyete proseem taksametr*
I'm in a hurry	**Spěchám**	*spyekhaam*
Stop here, please	**Zastavte tady prosím**	*zastavte tady proseem*
Wait a few minutes	**Počkejte pár minut**	*pochkeyte paar minut*
There is a mistake	**To není správně**	*to nenyee spraavnye*
On the meter it says 80 crowns	**Taxametr ukazuje osmdesát korun**	*taksametr ukazuye osmdesaat korun*
Can I have the receipt, please?	**Dejte mi prosím potvrzení**	*deyte mi proseem potvrzenyee*
Keep the change	**Drobné si nechte**	*drobnai si nekhte*
That's all right	**To je v pořádku**	*to ye fporzhaatku*

You may hear

Je to odsud ...	*ye to otsut*	It's ... away/from here
... deset kilometrů/půl hodiny	*deset kilometroo/pool hodyini*	... 10 kilometres/half an hour ...
Bude to stát ... korun	*bude to staat ... korun*	It will be ... crowns
Platí se příplatek ...	*platyee se przheeplatek*	There is a supplement ...
... za zavazadla	*za zavazadla*	... for the luggage

▌ The Czech Republic has a well-developed railway network so that you can reach practically any destination by train. It is, however, in need of some modernisation and travelling may not always be as comfortable as in the West – it is cheap compared to Western European standards, though.

▌ There are basically two types of train: the slower local train – **osobní vlak** – and the faster – **rychlík** (also called **expres**, or **spěšný vlak**). Intercity and Eurocity trains offer the highest standards. Local trains stop at all stations and have only standard or second-class cars. Fast trains stop only at larger cities and are equipped with sleepers and restaurant cars. On fast trains (marked in red on timetables) you can travel either first or second class.

▌ Sleepers are more comfortable (there are four people in a compartment) than couchettes (six in a compartment). Both must be booked in advance (up to 24 hours before the journey).

▌ Tickets can be bought at the station before the journey or in advance. Some travel agencies sell tickets for international trains. On busy routes it is advisable to buy a seat reservation (**místenka**) for a token amount after or when you buy a ticket.

▌ On some international or domestic fast trains it is compulsory to reserve a seat. On timetables these trains are distinguished by the letter 'R' in a box. If the 'R' is not boxed, seat reservations are available, but not compulsory. Carriages with reserved seats only are marked as **místenkový vůz** and are numbered. You may be fined if you are caught in a reserved-seats carriage without a seat reservation.

▌ Fast trains have numbers and some, operating on popular routes, also have names shown on the timetables. This is useful to know when buying tickets and making reservations.

▌ When buying tickets, you don't have to say that you want a single; if you simply say your destination, it will be assumed that you want a second-class single ticket on a local train. It is always a good idea to write down the relevant information if it is more complicated and hand it to the clerk.

∎ You cannot rely on staff at railway stations to speak English. During the holiday season information counters can be crowded, so it is better to use travel agencies to obtain information in advance.

∎ Timetables are not strictly adhered to. Allow extra time if you need to catch connecting trains.

∎ Note: you will notice that place names change their endings in a sentence, e.g. **Praha** (Prague), but **do Prahy** (to Prague), **v Praze** (in Prague) etc. You do not have to worry about the correct form to be understood and you will be able to recognise names, e.g. in station announcements, if you listen to the main part of the word and disregard the endings (see also BASIC GRAMMAR, page 12).

You may see

Čekárna	Waiting room	**Mezinárodní jízdenky**	International tickets
ČD	Czech railways		
Dámy	Ladies (toilets)	**Místenkový vůz**	Reserved seats only
Hlavní nádraží	Main railway station	**Místenky**	Seat reservations
Informace	Information	**Muži**	Men (toilets)
Jede ...	Runs on ... (followed by dates)	**Nejede ...**	Does not run on ... (dates)
Jen druhá třída	Second class only	**Odjezd vlaků**	Exit to platforms
Jídelní vůz	Restaurant car	**Odjezdy**	Departures
Jízdenky	Tickets	**Páni**	Gents (toilets)
Jízdní řád	Timetable	**Příjezdy**	Arrivals
Lehátkový vůz	Couchette car	**Rezervace**	Reservations
Lůžkový vůz	Sleeping car	**Směr**	Destination
		Úschovna zavazadel	Left-luggage office

Vnitrostátní jízdenky	Tickets for domestic routes	WC	Toilets
Výchdod	Exit	Záchody	Toilets
		Zpoždění	Delay

You may want to say

Information

Is there a train to Prague this evening/this afternoon/tomorrow morning?	**Jede dnes večer/dnes odpoledne/zítra ráno nějaký vlak do Prahy?**	*yede dnes vecher/ dnes dopoledne/zeetra raano nyeeakee vlak do prahi*
What time?	**V kolik hodin?**	*fkolik hodyin*
What time is the first/the next/the last train to Brno?	**V kolik (hodin) jede první/příští/poslední vlak do Brna?**	*fkolik (hodyin) yede prvnyee/przheeshtyee/ poslednyee vlak do brna*
What time does it arrive?	**V kolik (hodin) tam bude?**	*fkolik (hodyin) tam bude*
What time does the train from Prague arrive?	**V kolik (hodin) přijíždí vlak z Prahy?**	*fkolik (hodyin) przhiyeezhdyee vlak sprahi*
Is this the train to ... ?	**Je to vlak do ...?**	*ye to vlak do ...*
Which platform does the train to Plzeň leave from?	**Z kterého nástupiště odjíždí vlak do Plzně?**	*s kteraiho naastupishtye odyeezhdyee vlak do plznye*
Do I have to change trains?	**Musím přestupovat?**	*museem przhestupovat*
Where?	**Kde?**	*gde*
Do I have to ...	**Musím ...**	*museem*
Can I ...	**Můžu**	*moozhu*
... buy a seat reservation?	**... si koupit místenku?**	*si kohpit meestenku*
Is there a restaurant car?	**Má vlak jídelní vůz?**	*maa vlak yeedelnyee voos*

Tickets

(See also TIME, page 124)

One/Two for the fast train to Tábor, please	**Jeden/Dva na rychlík do Tábora**	*yeden/dva na rikhleek do taabora*
Single	**Jen tam**	*yen tam*
Return	**Zpáteční**	*spaatechnyee*
One adult/Two adults	**Jeden dospělý/ dva dospělí**	*yeden dospyelee/dva dospyelee*
(And) one child/two children	**(a) jedno dítě/dvě děti**	*(a) yedno dyeetye/dvye dyetyi*
For the Moravan (fast train)	**Na (rychlík) Moravan**	*na (rykhleek) moravan*
First/Second class	**První/Druhou třídu**	*prvnyee/druhoh trzheedu*
I'd like to reserve a seat/ two seats	**Místenku/Dvě místenky místenky prosím**	*meestenku/dvye meestenki proseem*
I'd like to reserve a sleeper/couchette	**Chtěl (male)/Chtěla (female) bych si rezervovat lůžko/ lehátko**	*khtyel/khtyela bikh si rezervovat looshko/lehaatko*
Can I take my bicycle on the train?	**Můžu si vzít do vlaku kolo?**	*moozhu si vzeet do vlaku kolo*
How much is it?	**Kolik to stojí?**	*kolik to stoyee*

Left-luggage

Can I leave this/these?	**Můžu tu tohle nechat?**	*moozhu tu tohle nekhat*
Until three o'clock	**Do tří hodin**	*do trzhee hodyin*
Until tomorrow	**Do zítřka**	*do zeetrzhka*
What time do you open/ close?	**Kdy otvíráte/zavíráte?**	*kdi otveeraate/ zaveeraate*
How much is it?	**Kolik to stojí?**	*kolik to stoyee*

On the train

I have reserved this seat	**Mám na tohle místo místenku**	*maam na tohle meesto meestenku*

Is this seat taken?	**Je tohle místo obsazeno?**	*ye tohle **mees**to **op**sazeno*
Are there any free seats here?	**Jsou tu nějaká volná místa?**	*ysoh tu nyeyakaa **vol**naa **mees**ta*
Do you mind if I ...?	**Bude vám vadit, když ...?**	*bude vaam **va**dyit gdish*
... open/close the window	**... otevřu/zavřu okno**	*otevrzhu/ **zav**rzhu **ok**no*
... smoke	**... si zapálím**	*si **za**paaleem*
Where is ...?	**Kde je ...?**	*gde ye*
... the sleeping car	**... lůžkový vůz**	***loosh**kovee **voos***
... the car with reserved seats number ...	**... místenkový vůz číslo ...**	***mees**tenkovee **voos** cheeslo ...*
... the restaurant car	**... jídelní vůz**	*yeedelnyee **voos***
Excuse me, may I get past?	**Dovolíte?/S dovolením**	*dovoleete/ **zdo**volenyeem*
Can you tell me ...?	**Můžete mi říct, ...?**	*moozhete mi **rzheetst***
... where we are	**... kde jsme**	*gde **ysme***
... how long the train stops here	**... jak dlouho tu vlak stojí**	*yak dloh-ho tu **vlak** stoyee*
... when we get to České Budějovice	**... kdy se dostaneme do Českých Budějovic?**	*gdi se **do**staneme do cheskeekh budyeyovits*
Is this Písek?	**Je to Písek?**	*ye to **pee**sek*

You may hear

Information

(See also TIME, page 124)

Osobní vlak/rychlík do ...	*osobnyee **vlak do***	The local train to ...
...odjíždí z nástupiště ...	*odyeezhdyee z **naa**stupishtye*	... leaves from platform (number) ...
...přijede na nástupiště ...	*przhiyede na **naa**stupishtye*	... arrives at platform (number) ...

Ukončete nástup do rychlíku Smetana	*ukonchete naastup do rikhleeku smetana*	All aboard, please, for the Smetana fast train
Expres je k odjezdu připraven ...	*ekspres ye k odyezdu przhipraven*	The express is due to leave ...
... na nástupišti ...	*na naastupishtyi*	... from platform (number)
Upozornění pro cestující	*upozornyenyee pro tsestuyeetsee*	Passenger announcement
Rychlík z ... do ...	*rikhleek z ... do ...*	The fast train from ... to ...
... pravidelný příjezd/ odjezd ...	*pravidelnee przheeyest/ odyest*	... with regular arrival/ departure ...
...má zpoždění	*(maa spozhdyenyee)*	... is delayed
... je asi třicet minut opožděn.	*ye asi trzhitset minut opozhdyen*	... is about 30 minutes late

Tickets

(See also TIME, page 124)

Na kdy chcete jízdenku?	*na gdi khtsete yeezdenku*	When do you want to travel?
Kdy se vracíte?	*gdi se vratseete*	When do you want to come back?
Kuřáci nebo nekuřáci?	*kurzhaatsi nebo nekurzhaatsi*	Smoking or non-smoking?
Místenky jsou vyprodány	*meestenki ysoh viprodaani*	There are no reserved seats left
Lůžka/lehátka jsou bohužel vyprodána	*looshka/lehaatka ysoh bohuzhel viprodaana*	I'm sorry, there are no sleepers/ couchettes left
Máme jen první třídu	*maame yen prvnyee trzheedu*	There is only first class left
Musíte mít místenku	*museete meet meestenku*	You must reserve a seat
Je to místenkový vlak.	*ye to meestenkovee vlak*	This train is reserved seats only
Musíte přesedat/ přestupovat v ...	*museete przhesedat/przhestupovat v*	You have to change in ...

■ The Czech Republic has coach connections with all European capitals and a dense domestic network of bus lines. The main coach terminal is Praha-Florenc, serving all international and long-distance internal routes.

■ Most domestic lines are run by the Czech national coach company, ČSAD. Some popular long-distance domestic routes are also served by private companies.

■ Most towns have public bus transport systems. Tickets are available at newsagents', or tobacconists', and in large cities from ticket machines. The same type of ticket can usually be used for other forms of local public transport (see UNDERGROUND TRAVEL, page 55). In Prague and Brno tourist passes (**turistická síťová jízdenka**) valid for up to five days can be bought.

■ Tickets, which are valid for one ride, have to be validated on boarding the bus by punching them at a machine. On-the-spot fines are issued if passengers are caught without a valid ticket. Public tram and trolley bus systems operate on the same principles.

You may see

Autobusové nádraží	Bus/Coach station
ČSAD	Czech national coach company
Jízdenky	Tickets
Městská hromadná doprava/MHD	Municipal transport system
Mezinárodní linky/spoje	International connections
Seznam linek	List of connections
Služební jízda	Not in service
Stání/Nástupní stanice (číslo...)	Boarding stop (number ...) at a coach station
Vnitrostátní linky/spoje	National connections

| Zákaz kouření | No smoking |
| Zastávka na znamení | Request stop |

In the timetable

Jede ...	Runs on ... (followed by signs or dates)
Nejede ...	Does not run on ... (followed by signs or dates)
Denně kromě ...	Daily except ...
... soboty/neděle/ státem uznávaných svátků	... Saturdays/Sundays/public holidays
Jezdí jen ...	Runs on ... only
... v pracovní dny/ve dnech pracovního klidu/v neděli	... on workdays/holidays/Sundays ...

You may want to say

Information

Where do I catch a bus ...?	**Odkud jede autobus ...?**	*otkut yede autobus*
What number is the bus ...?	**Které číslo autobusu jede ...?**	*kterai cheeslo autobusu yede*
What time is the first/ the next/the last bus ...?	**V kolik jede první /příští/poslední autobus ...**	*fkolik yede prvnyee/ przheeshtyee/poslednyee autobus*
... to the railway station	**... k nádraží**	*k naadrazhee*
... to the city centre	**... do centra**	*do tsentra*
... to the airport	**... na letiště**	*na letyishtye*
What time does it arrive there?	**V kolik tam bude?**	*fkolik tam bude*
Which platform?	**Které je to nástupiště?**	*kterai ye to naastupishtye*
Does the bus (to) ... leave from here?	**Odjíždí odsud autobus (do/k/na) ...?**	*odyeezhdyee otsut autobus do/k/na*

53

Where is the stop for the (tram/bus number) four/ten?	Kde je zastávka čtyřky/desítky?	gde ye zastaafka chtyrzhki/deseetki
Is this the bus/tram (to) ...?	Je to autobus/tramvaj (do/k/na) ...?	ye to autobus/tramvay do/k/na ...
I want to get off ...	Chci vystoupit ...	khtsi vistohpit ...
... at the museum	... u muzea	u muzea
... at the station	... u nádraží	u naadrazhee
Please tell me where to get off	Řekněte mi prosím, kde mám vystoupit	rzheknyete mi proseem gde maam vistohpit
Excuse me, may I get past?	Dovolíte?	dovoleete

Tickets

One/Two tickets	Jednu jízdenku/Dvě jízdenky	yednu yeezdenku/dvye yeezdenki
For an adult/a child	Pro dospělého/dítě	pro dospelaiho/dyeetye
Where can I buy a tourist network pass?	Kde dostanu turistickou síťovou jízdenku?	gde dostanu turistitskoh seetyovoh yeezdenku
Twenty tickets, please	Dvacet jizdenek prosím	dvatset yeezdenek proseem
How much is it?	Kolik to stojí?	kolik to stoyee

You may hear

Autobus do centra jede ...	autobus do tsentra yede	The bus to the city/town centre leaves ...
... z této/vedlejší zastávky/	s taito/vedleyshee zastaafki/	... from this/the next stop/the stop
ze zastávky naproti	ze zastaafki naprotyi	across the street
Jezdí každých deset minut	yezdye kazhdeekh deset minut	They go every 10 minutes
Odjíždí za půl hodiny	odyeezhdyee za pool hodyini	It leaves in half an hour

■ Prague's underground railway (**metro**) forms the backbone of the public transport system in the capital. It is convenient, efficient and clean. There are bus connections linking the metro stations with other parts of the city. Some metro stations are conveniently situated near some of Prague's most famous sights.

■ The metro system has three lines distinguished by different colours on the metro map: the green A line (**trasa A**), the yellow B line (**trasa B**), and the red C line (**trasa C**). There are three metro junctions (**přestupní stanice**) in the city centre. The underground runs from 5 a.m. until midnight every day.

■ Tickets (**jízdenky**) for the underground (valid for other means of municipal transportation) must be bought in advance. They are available from tobacconists' (**tabák**), newsagents and kiosks, some food shops, and at yellow ticket machines near metro entrances. A tourist pass (**turistická síťová jízdenka**) valid from one to five days allows unlimited travel on all means of municipal transport and can be bought at some newsagents in the city centre and from multilingual machines at certain metro stations.

■ Tickets must be validated before the journey at one of the stamping machines at the top of the escalators. They are valid for any destination and can be used for one hour, provided you do not leave the underground. Fares are displayed near the entrance to the underground. Plain-clothes inspectors identifying themselves by showing a badge carry out random checks. If you are caught without a valid ticket, you may have to pay an instant fine.

■ Signs on platforms indicate the name of the final station (**stanice**) of the trains running in both directions (**směr**).

■ Underground stations are marked with green signs with the letter M within an upside down triangle. On public bus and tram timetables connections to the metro are marked by the letter 'M'.

You may see

Jízdenky	Tickets
MHD	Municipal public transport
Předprodej jízdenek	Tickets sold here
Přestup	Station where you can transfer to other lines
Směr	Direction
Stanice	Station
Turistické jízdenky	Tourist passes
Výstup	Exit

You may want to say

Do you have a map of the underground?	Máte plánek metra?	*maate plaanek metra*
Where can I buy tickets for the underground?	Kde se kupují jízdenky na metro?	*gde se kupuyee yeezdenki na metro*
Where is the nearest underground station?	Kde je nejbližší stanice metra?	*gde ye neyblishee stanyitse metra*
Which line is it for the Old Town Square/Petřín View Tower/Lesser Town?	Kterou trasou se dostanu na Staroměstské náměstí/ k Petřínské rozhledně/ na Malou stranu?	*kteroh trasoh se dostanu na staromyestskai naamnyestyee/ kpetrzheenskai rozhlednye/na maloh stranu*
Which stop is it for Prague Castle/the Charles Bridge/ the National Theatre?	Která zastávka je na Hrad/na Karlův most/ k Národnímu divadlu?	*kteraa zastaafka ye na hrat/na karloof most/ k naarodnyeemu dyivadlu*
Where are we?	Kde jsme?	*gde ysme*
Show me on the map, please	Kde je to na mapě prosím?	*gde ye to na mapye proseem*

56

| Is this the right stop for Wenceslas Square? | je to správná stanice na Václavské náměstí? | ye to spraavnaa stanyitse na vaatslafskai naamnyestyee |
| Which direction is it for the city centre? | Kterým směrem je to do centra? | ktereem smnyerem ye to do tsentra |

You may hear

Vaše jízdenky prosím/ Kontrola jízdenek	vashe yeezdenki proseem/kontrola yeezdenek	Your tickets, please/Can I see your ticket, please?
Ukončete prosím výstup a nástup, dveře se zavírají	ukonchete proseem veestupa naastup dverzhe se zaveerayee	Stand clear of the door, please, the door is about to close
Příští stanice – Můstek	przeeshtyee stanyitse moostek	The next station is Můstek
Přestup na trasu A	przhestup na trasu aa	Change here for line A
Konečná	konechnaa	This is the last stop
Prosíme vystupte	proseeme vistupte	All change, please
Ustupte prosím za bezpečnostní pás	ustupte proseem za bespechnostnyee paas	Please stand behind the safety line

Air travel

▮ If you travel by air, you will arrive at the Czech Republic's only international airport at Ruzyně, which is about 15 kilometres from the centre of Prague.

▮ There are daily scheduled flights into Prague by Czechoslovak Airlines (CSA) and British Airways and charter flights by all major international carriers. There are direct flights between Prague-Ruzyně and most major European cities, New York and Montreal. There are one- and two-stop flights from other US cities.

▮ The small Ruzyně airport is equipped with all the necessary facilities. All major credit cards are accepted. English is generally spoken at the counters and all important signs are in both Czech and English.

▮ The airport tax (about £5) is normally included in the price of any ticket bought from a travel agency. It is advisable to reconfirm your booking directly with the airline company three days before departure.

▮ CSA runs a regular bus and car service to the city centre. In addition, you can use cheap public transport buses which stop right in front of the airport building. One of the bus lines will take you to an underground terminus. Taxis are the most expensive alternative and it is advisable to agree the fare in advance.

You may see

Bezcelní odbavení	Nothing to declare
Doprava do města letištními vozy	Transport to the city centre by airport cars
K proclení	Goods to declare
Letiště	Airport
Nástupní	Bus stop (where you board)

Nouzový východ	Emergency exit
Odlet	Departures
Odbavení (zavazadel)	(Luggage) check-in
Pasová/celní kontrola	Passport/Customs check-in
Pronájem automobilů	Car hire
Přílet	Arrivals
Směnárna	Bureau de change
Úschovna zavazadel	Left-luggage office
Výdej zavazadel	Baggage reclaim
Východ	Gate/Exit
Výstupní	Bus stop (where you alight)
WC	Toilets
Zákaz kouření	No smoking
Zboží k proclení	Goods to declare
Zpoždění	Delay

You may want to say

Is there a flight from Prague to Brno?	**Letí něco z Prahy do Brna?**	*letyee nyetso sprahi do brna*
What time is the first/the next/the last flight ...	**Kdy letí první/příští/poslední letadlo ...**	*gdi letyee prvnyee/przheeshtyee/poslednyee letadlo*
... to London/New York/Montreal?	**... do Londýna/New Yorku/Montrealu?**	*do londeena/nyu yorku/montriyawlu*
What time does it arrive in Prague?	**Kdy přilétá do Prahy?**	*gdi przhilaitaa do prahi*
A ticket/Two tickets to Vienna/Frankfurt/Zurich	**Letenku/Dvě letenky do Vídně/Frankfurtu/Curychu**	*letenku/dvye letenki do veednye/frankfurtu/tsurikhu*
Return	**Zpáteční**	*spaatechnyee*
1st class/Business class	**První třída**	*prvnyee trzheeda*

Economy class	**Turistická třída**	*turistitskaa trzhee*da
By the window, please	**U okna prosím**	*u okna proseem*
In the aisle, please	**V uličce prosím**	*f ulichtse proseem*
Smoking, please	**Kuřáci prosím**	*kurzhaatsi proseeem*
Non-smoking, please	**Nekuřáci prosím**	*nekurzhaatsi proseem*
I'd like to change/cancel my reservation	**Chtěl** (male)/**Chtěla** (female) **bych změnit/ zrušit svou rezervaci**	*khtyel/khtye*la bikh *zmnyenyit/zrushit svoh rezervatsi*
What is the flight number?	**Jaké je číslo letu?**	*yakai ye chee*slo *letu*
What time do I have to check in?	**Kdy musím přijít k odbavení?**	*gdi museem przhiyeet k od*bavenyee
Which gate is it?	**Který východ?**	*kteree veekhod*
Is the flight to Vienna/ London delayed?	**Má let do Vídně/ Londýna zpoždění?**	*maa let do veednye/ londeena spozhdyenyee*
Where is the luggage from the London flight?	**Kde jsou zavazadla z Londýna?**	*gde ysoh zavazadla z londeena*
My luggage is not here	**Mé zavazadlo tu není**	*mai zavazadlo tu nenyee*

You may hear

U okna nebo v uličce?	*u okna nebo f ulichtse*	By the window or in the aisle?
Kuřáci nebo nekuřáci?	*kurzhaatsi nebo nekurzhaatsi*	Smoking or non-smoking?
Váš pas prosím.	*vaash pas proseem*	Your passport, please
Máte něco k proclení?	*maate nyetso k protslenyee*	Do you have any goods to declare?
Dostavte se k odbavení dvě hodiny před odletem	*dostafte se k od*bavenyee *dvye* hodyini *przhet odletem*	Please check in two hours before departure
Let má dvě hodiny zpoždění	*let maa dvye hodyini spozhd*yenyee	The plane is delayed by two hours
Váš palubní lístek prosím	*vaash palubnyee lees*tek *proseem*	Boarding pass, please

At the tourist office

■ (See also DIRECTIONS, page 33, ACCOMMODATION, page 63, USEFUL ADDRESSES, page 137)

■ In Prague, general and tourist information can be obtained at one of the offices of **Pražská informační služba** (Prague Information Service) or **PIS** located in the city centre. A number of travel agencies provide information on transport, accommodation and tours, as well as services for tourists. The largest, the **Čedok** travel agency with English-speaking staff, has several offices in the city centre. **Česká centrála turistického ruchu** (Czech tourism centre) has a selection of tourist leaflets.

■ Some larger cities also have their own tourist offices which offer advice and sell maps and guide books. Tourist information is sometimes offered at railway and coach stations. Look for the **i** sign in a blue square. Most towns and cities have branches of Čedok and other travel agencies where information can be found. Local bookshops will sell regional maps and town plans.

You may want to say

Where is the tourist information office?	**Kde je turistická informační kancelář?**	*gde* ye *turistitskaa informachnyee kantselaarzh*
Do you speak English?	**Mluvíte anglicky?**	*mluveete anglitski*
Do you have ...?	**Máte ... ?**	*maate*
... a plan of the town	**... plánek města**	*plaanek mnyesta*
... a map of the area	**... mapu okolí**	*mapu okolee*
... a list of hotels	**... seznam hotelů**	*seznam hoteloo*
Can you recommend ...?	**Můžete mi doporučit ...?**	*moozhete mi doporuchit*
... a cheap hotel	**... levný hotel**	*levnee hotel*

At the tourist office

... a hotel in the city centre	... nějaký hotel v centru	nyeyakee hotel f tsentru
... a traditional restaurant	... nějakou tradiční restauraci	nyeyakoh tradichnyee restauratsi
... bed-and-breakfast accommodation	... ubytování se snídaní	ubitovaanyee se snyeedaanyee
... an interesting trip	... zajímavý výlet	zayeemavee veelet
Can you book a hotel for me, please?	Můžete mi zamluvit hotel prosím?	moozhete mi zamluvit hotel proseem
Where can I/we hire a car?	Kde se dá najmout auto?	gde se daa naymoht auto
What is there to see here?	Co se tu dá vidět?	tso se tu daa vidyet
Do you have information about ...?	Máte informace o ...	maate informatse o
... train/bus connections	... vlakovém/ autobusovém spojení	vlakovaim/autobusovaim spoyenyee
... sights in the area	... památkách v okolí	pamaatkaakh f okolee
Can you show me on the map?	Můžete mi to ukázat na mapě?	moozhete mi to ukaazat na mapye
When is the museum open?	Kdy je muzeum otevřeno?	gdi ye muzeum otevrzheno
Are there any excursions?	Máte nějaké výlety?	maate nyeyakai veeleti

You may hear

Co si přejete?	tso si przheyete	Can I help you?
Odkud jste?	otkut yste	Where are you from?
Pro kolik osob?	pro kolik osop	For how many people?
Na jak dlouho?	na yak dloh-ho	For how long?
Prosím	proseem	Here you are

Accommodation

▌ Accommodation can be arranged either independently or through an accommodation/travel agency for a fee. Some hotels have a contracted room allocation with a travel agency (e.g. **Čedok** with branches abroad – see USEFUL ADDRESSES, page 137). It is advisable to book in advance for the peak seasons: the summer months and the Christmas and Easter holidays. Prague offers accommodation in all price categories, with perhaps less choice in budget hotels.

▌ The various types of accommodation are:

- hotels (**hotel**). There is no unified hotel classification, although the old system consisting of the **A, B,** and **C** categories is being increasingly replaced by the star system. International chains are represented. Breakfast is not normally included in the price of a hotel room.

- guest houses (**penzión**). These are often private houses converted into apartment blocks or with rooms fitted out with extra facilities. They may provide more personal, though not always cheaper, accommodation than a hotel.

- hostels (**turistická ubytovna**) provide a budget-type of accommodation of variable standard, often with shared amenities. Some youth hostels (**mládežnická ubytovna**) run by the **CKM** (Youth Travel Agency affiliated to the International Youth Hostel Federation IYHF) are very good value. Student dormitories (**studentská kolej**) open to tourists during the summer months are quite comfortable but often booked up in advance by groups.

- private rooms (**pokoj, bydlení v soukromí, privát**). Renting a room in somebody else's home is more expensive if you are looking for a central location.

- campsites (**kemp, autokemping**) open from spring to autumn. Most are equipped with basic amenities. Campsites in and around the capital tend to be much more expensive than those in more remote parts of the country.

▌ Voltage is 220 V all over the Czech Republic. Plugs with two or three round pins are required (British and US appliances need a travel adaptor).

Information requested on a registration card

Jméno	First name	**Místo narození**	Place of birth
Příjmení	Surname	**Pas číslo**	Passport number
Národnost	Nationality	**Vydán**	Issued at
Povolání	Occupation	**Datum**	Date
Datum narození	Date of birth	**Podpis**	Signature

You may see

Horská chata	Mountain hut	**Prádelna**	Laundry
Jídelna	Dining room	**Recepce**	Reception
Kemp(ing)	Campsite	**Sprchy**	Showers
Koupelna	Bathroom	**Stany**	Tents
Nouzový východ	Emergency exit	**Studentská kolej**	Student hostel
Obsazeno	No vacancies	**Umývárna**	Lavatory/Washroom
Penzión	Guest house	**Voda není pitná**	Non-drinking water
Pitná voda	Drinking water	**Volné pokoje**	Vacancies
Plavecký bazén	Swimming pool	**Výtahy**	Lifts
Plná penze	Full board	**WC/Záchody**	Toilets
Pokoj k pronajmutí	A room to let		
Polopenze	Half-board		

You may want to say

Booking in and out

I've reserved a room	**Mám rezervovaný pokoj**	*maam rezervovanee pokoy*
My name is ...	**Jmenuji se ...**	*ymenuyi se*
Do you have a room?	**Máte volný pokoj?**	*maate volnee pokoy*
A single room	**Jednolůžkový pokoj**	*yednolooshkovee pokoy*
A double room	**Pokoj s dvoulůžkem**	*pokoy s dvohlooshkem*
A twin room	**Dvoulůžkový pokoj**	*dvohlooshkovee pokoy*
For one night/two nights	**Na jednu noc/dvě noci**	*na yednu nots/dvye notsi*
A room ...	**Pokoj ...**	*pokoy*
.. with a shower/ with a bathroom/ with a bath and a toilet	**... se sprchou/ s koupelnou/ s příslušenstvím**	*se sprkhoh/s kohpelnoh/ s przheeslushenstveem*
Can I see the room?	**Můžu ten pokoj vidět?**	*moozhu ten pokoy vidyet*
Do you have space for a tent/caravan?	**Máte místo pro stan/ karavan?**	*maate meesto pro stan/ karavan*
How much is it?	**Kolik to stojí?**	*kolik to stoyee*
Per night/week	**Za noc/týden**	*za nots/teeden*
Is there a reduction for children?	**Je na děti sleva?**	*ye na dyetyi sleva*
Is breakfast included?	**Je v tom snídaně?**	*ye ftom snyeedanye*
It's too expensive	**To je moc drahé**	*to ye mots drahai*
Do you have anything cheaper?	**Máte něco levnějšího?**	*maate nyetso levnyeysheeho*
Do you have anything bigger/smaller?	**Máte něco většího/ menšího?**	*maate nyetso vyetsheeho/ mensheeho*
I'd like to stay another night	**Rád bych zůstal ještě jednu noc**	*raad bikh zoostal yeshtye yednu nots*
I'm leaving tomorrow morning	**Odjíždím zítra ráno**	*odyeezhdyeem zeetra raano*
The bill, please	**Účet prosím**	*oochet proseem*

Do you take credit cards/traveller's cheques?	**Berete kreditní karty/ cestovní šeky?**	*berete kreditnyee karti/ tsestovnyee sheki*
Can you recommend a hotel/cheap hotel/good hotel?	**Můžete doporučit nějaký hotel/levný hotel/dobrý hotel?**	*moozhete doporuchit nyeyakee hotel/levnee hotel/dobree hotel*
Can you phone them to make a booking, please?	**Můžete tam zavolat a rezervovat mi pokoj?**	*moozhete tam zavolat a rezervovat mi pokoy*

In hotels

(See also PROBLEMS AND COMPLAINTS, page 113)

Where can we park?	**Kde můžeme zaparkovat?**	*gde moozheme zaparkovat*
Do you have a cot for the baby?	**Máte dětskou postýlku?**	*maate dyetskoh posteelku*
Is there room service?	**Je tu hotelová obsluha?**	*ye tu hotelovaa opsluha*
Do you have facilities for the disabled?	**Máte vybavení pro tělesně postižené?**	*maate vibavenyee pro tyelesnye postizhenai*
What time is breakfast/ lunch/dinner?	**Kdy se podává snídaně/ oběd/večeře?**	*gdi se podaavaa snyeedanye/obyet/ vecherzhe*
Can I/we have breakfast in the room?	**Mohu dostat snídani na pokoj?**	*mohu dostat snyeedanyi na pokoy*
I'll be back very late	**Vrátím se velmi pozdě**	*vraatyeem se velmi pozdye*
(Key) number ... , please	**(Klíč) číslo ... prosím.**	*kleech cheeslo ... proseem*
Are there any messages for me?	**Mám tu nějaké vzkazy?**	*maam tu nyeyakai fskazi*
Where is the bathroom?	**Kde je koupelna?**	*gde ye kohpelna*
Can I leave this in the safe?	**Uložíte mi to do sejfu?**	*ulozheete mi to do seyfu*
Can I have my things from the safe?	**Vrátíte mi mé věci ze sejfu?**	*vraatyeete mi mai vyetsi ze seyfu*
Can you call me at eight o'clock?	**Můžete mě vzbudit v osm hodin?**	*moozhete mnye vzbudyit f osm hodyin*

Can you order me a taxi?	Můžete mi objednat taxi?	*moozhete mi obyednat taxi*
For right now	Na teď	*na tety*
For tomorrow at nine o'clock	Zítra na devátou hodinu	*zeetra na devaatoh hodyinu*
Can you find me a babysitter?	Můžete mi najít hlídání k dítěti (child)/ k dětem (children)?	*moozhete mi nayeet hleedaanye g dyeetyety/ g dyetem*
Can you put it on the bill?	Můžete mi to připsat na účet?	*moozhete mi to przhipsat na oochet*
Room number ...	Pokoj číslo ...	*pokoy cheeslo*

At campsites

Is there a campsite near here?	Je tu někde kemp(ing)?	*ye tu nyegde kempink*
Can I/we camp here?	Smí se tu stanovat?	*smee se tu stanovat*
Where can I/we park?	Kde se dá parkovat?	*gde se daa parkovat*
Where are the showers/ toilets/dustbins?	Kde jsou sprchy/záchody/ nádoby na odpadky?	*gde ysoh sprkhi/ zaakhodi/naadobi na otpatki*
Is the water drinkable?	Je to pitná voda?	*ye to pitnaa voda*
Where is the laundry-room?	Kde je prádelna?	*gde ye praadelna*
Where is there a power point?	Kde je elektrická přípojka?	*gde ye elektritskaa przheepoyka*

Self-catering accommodation

(See also DIRECTIONS, page 33, and PROBLEMS AND COMPLAINTS, page 113)

I have rented a house/ an apartment	Najal jsem si dům/byt	*nayal ysem si doom/bit*
My name is ...	Jmenuji se ...	*ymenuyi se*
What is the address?	Jaká je adresa?	*yakaa ye adresa*
How do I get there?	Jak se tam dostanu?	*yak se tam dostanu*

Can you give me the key?	Můžete mi dát klíč?	*moozhete mi daat kleech*
Where is ...?	Kde je ... ?	*gde ye*
Where is the wardrobe?	Kde je skříň na šaty?	*gde ye skrzheeny na shati*
Where is the fuse box?	Kde jsou pojistky?	*gde ysoh poyistki*
How does the cooker work?	Jak se zapíná ten vařič?	*yak se zapeenaa ten varzhich*
How does the water heater work?	Jak se zapíná ten ohřívač vody?	*yak se zapeenaa ten ohrzheevach vodi*
Is there a spare gas bottle?	Je tu náhradní plynová bomba?	*ye tu naahradnyee plinovaa bomba*
Is there any spare bedding?	Je tu náhradní povlečení?	*ye tu naahradnyee povlechenyee*
What day do they come to clean?	Který den se uklízí?	*kteree den se ukleezee*
Where do I/we put the rubbish?	Kam se dávají odpadky?	*kam se daavayee otpatki*

You may hear

Budete si přát?/ Jaké máte přání?	*budete si przhaat/yakai maate przhaanyee*	Can I help you?
Čím posloužím?	*cheem poslohzheem*	What can I do for you?
Je mi líto, máme obsazeno	*ye mi leeto maame opsazeno*	I'm sorry, we're full
Na kolik dní?	*na kolik dnyee*	For how many days?
Pro kolik osob?	*pro kolik osop*	For how many people?

Telephones

▌ Digital card and coin-operated phone boxes for national and international calls are now widely in use in Prague and some larger towns.

▌ Phone cards (**telefonní karta**) for both local and international calls can be bought at post offices, newsagents and Czech Telecom shops. To make a call from a new-style card or coin-operated phone box follow the picture instructions or those on the display (an English translation is available by pressing a button on some phones).

▌ The dialling tone is a sequence of long and short notes (· – · – · –), the ringing tone consists of regular long notes (– – – –) and if the number is engaged you will hear repeated stacatto notes (· · · ·). Three tones of varying pitch indicate that the number is no longer in service or that there is a technical problem.

▌ The older coin-operated phone boxes use only low denomination coins and should not be used for international calls.

▌ At the time of writing, the entire telephone system is being completely modernised, so be prepared for occasional problems getting through or numbers changing.

▌ Sometimes it may be easier to book an international call at a post office (you pay a deposit at the counter and then dial direct from a specified booth) or to use a private phone. Hotels charge a supplement.

▌ Prague's main post office (**Hlavní pošta**) is located in the city centre in Jindřišská street near Wenceslas Square. It is open 24 hours a day and has non-stop international phone, fax and telex facilities. Post offices in larger towns provide international phone and fax services during usual opening hours. All large towns have at least one post office open 24 hours a day.

▌ For important telephone numbers see USEFUL AND EMERGENCY TELEPHONE NUMBERS, page 139.

Instructions you may see in the phone box

Sejměte sluchátko	*seymnyete slukhaatko*	Lift the handset
Vhoďte mince	*vhodyte mintse*	Insert coins
Vložte telefonní kartu	*vloshte telefonyee kartu*	Insert phone card
Volte číslo	*volte cheeslo*	Dial the number
Vyjměte kartu	*viymnyete kartu*	Remove phone card

You may see

Hasiči	Fire brigade
Městská policie	Municipal police
Meziměstský hovor	National call
Mezistátní hovor	International call
Mimo provoz	Out of order
Místní hovor	Local call
Na účet volaného	Collect/Reverse charge call
Národní směrové číslo	Area/City code
Policie	Police
Prodej telefonních karet	Phone cards sold here
Silniční a havarijní sužba	Road and car breakdown service
Směrové číslo země	International code
Telefonní seznam	Telephone directory
Záchranná služba	Ambulance
Zlaté stránky	Yellow pages

You may want to say

(See also NUMBERS, page 121)

| Where is the telephone? | **Kde je telefon?** | *gde ye telefon* |

Is there a payphone near here?	Je tu někde telefon na mince?	ye tu nyegde telefon namintse
Do you have change for the telephone, please?	Měl (you=male)/ Měla (you=female) byste drobné na telefon?	mnyel/mnyela biste drobnai ha telefon
Where can I get a phone card?	Kde dostanu telefonní kartu?	gde dostanu telefonyee kartu
Do you have a telephone directory?	Máte telefonní seznam?	maate telefonyee seznam
I'd like to call England/ Prague	Chci zavolat do Anglie/ do Prahy	khtsi zavolat do angliye/do prahi
The number is ...	Na číslo ...	na cheeslo
Collect/Reverse charge	Na účet volaného	na oochet volanaiho
Extension ... please	Linku ... prosím	linku ... proseem
My name is ...	Jmenuji se ...	ymenuyi se
It's ... speaking	U telefonu je ...	u telefonu ye
Can I speak to ...?	Můžu mluvit s ...?	moozhu mluvit s
When will he/she be back?	Kdy se vrátí?	kdi se vraatyee
I'll call again later	Zavolám později	zavolaam pozdyeyi
Can I leave a message?	Můžu nechat vzkaz?	moozhu nekhat fskas
Please tell him/her ...	Můžete mu/jí říct, ...	moozhete mu/yee rzheetst
... that I called	...že jsem volal (I=male)/ volala (I=female)?	zhe ysem volal/volala
... that I'm at the Evropa Hotel	...že jsem v hotelu Evropa?	zhe ysem v hotelu evropa
... to call me back	... aby mi zavolal (he is to call) /zavolala (she is to call)	abi mi zavolal/ zavolala
I'll wait	Počkám	pochkaam
My telephone number is ...	Moje telefonní číslo je ...	moye telefonyee cheeslo ye

71

Can you repeat that, please?	Můžete to prosím opakovat?	moozhete to proseem opakovat
More slowly, please	Pomaleji prosím	pomaleyi proseem
Sorry, I've got the wrong number	Promiňte, mám špatné číslo	prominyte maam shpatnai cheeslo
We've been cut off	Byli jsme přerušeni	bili ysme przherushenyi
How much is the call?	Kolik stojí ten hovor?	kolik stoyee ten hovor

You may hear

Prosím	proseem	Hello? (said by person answering the phone)
U telefonu	u telefonu	Speaking
Není doma/tu	nenyee doma/tu	He/She isn't in
Vrátí se zítra	vraatyee se zeetra	He/She'll be back tomorrow
Kdo volá?	gdo volaa	Who's calling?
Mám/Můžu něco vyřídit?	maam/moozhu nyetso virzheedyit	Shall/Can I take a message?
Okamžik, přepojím	okamzhik przhepoyeem	One moment, I'm putting you through
Je obsazeno	ye opsazeno	The line is engaged
Koho voláte?	koho volaate	Who are you calling?
Promiňte, to je omyl	prominyte to ye omyl	Sorry, wrong number
Záloha je 30 korun	zaaloha ye trzhitset korun	The deposit is 30 crowns
Kabina číslo 4	kabina cheeslo chtirzhi	Booth number four

Eating and drinking

▌ There is a variety of places to go for a full meal:

- pubs (**hospoda**) and taverns (**hostinec**) usually serve traditional Czech fare. A full meal is often served at beer halls (**pivnice**) frequented by locals usually to drink good draught beer.

- restaurants (**restaurace**) offer a wide variety of local, international and special national cuisines. There is not a clear distinction between a pub and a restaurant.

- wine bars and wine cellars (**vinárna, vinný sklípek**) offer anything from snacks to a complete menu along with a choice of wines and drinks. Beer is normally only served with meals.

▌ A limited choice of hot dishes and soups for an unpretentious customer is also available at stand-up snack bars or self-service cafeterias (**bufet, automat, jídelna**).

▌ Cafés and coffee bars (**kavárna**) will mostly only serve cold snacks, pastries and cakes to go with a variety of coffees, soft and alcoholic drinks. Coffee (**káva**) will be served black unless you ask for milk (**s mlékem**). Unfiltered coffee with the grains at the bottom is still common in pubs and some other places. If you want filtered coffee, ask for an espresso (**espreso, preso**).

▌ Fast food (**rychlé občerstvení**) is available at street kiosks and snack bars (**bufet, občerstvení**) which sometimes adjoin food shops (e.g. delicatessen or cured meat counters). Dairy specialities, milkshakes and pastries are on offer at milk bars (**mléčný bar**). Cold meats, open sandwiches (**chlebíčky**), salads (**saláty**) and the traditional boiled or grilled sausages (**klobásy**) and Frankfurters (**párky**) with mustard are the most common fare. Western-style fast food, such as pizzas, hamburgers and hot dogs, is increasingly popular.

▌ All types of restaurants are divided into four price categories (**cenová skupina** I – IV, I being the best), which are normally indicated on the menu.

■ Traditional Czech cuisine is rich and based on meat; vegetarians and vegans are not well catered for and meatless dishes are not necessarily suitable for vegetarians. Fish is not often found on menus and will mostly include cod fillet, or local freshwater fish like carp or trout. Up-market restaurants however do serve a wider variety of fish, including seafood. Sweet dishes are sometimes served as main courses.

■ Beer drinkers will definitely come into their own in Czech beer halls. Beer (**pivo**) comes in two varieties – light (**světlé**) and dark (**černé**) – and in different strengths: the two most common are 10-degree (**desítka**) and 12-degree (**dvanáctka**). This, however, does not indicate the alcohol volume, which for most beers is between four and six percent. If you ask for a large (**velké**) beer, you get half a litre; small (**malé**) means about a third of a litre. **řezané pivo** is a mixture of light and dark beer.

■ In a traditional beer hall, you will be served at the table and your empty glass will automatically be exchanged for a full one until you indicate that you do not want to drink any more. The waiter will mark down what you have on a slip of paper left on your table. When settling the bill, you will be expected to leave a tip. Either round up the amount to the nearest 10 or say how much you intend to pay.

■ Among the locally produced wines, some Moravian labels are considered good quality. Wines are ordered in restaurants by the bottle (**sedmička**, i.e. 75 cl), by the glass (**sklenka** or **dvě deci**, which is two decilitres) or, often in a wine bar, by the jug (**džbánek**).

■ Service is usually included in the price but a tip of between five and 15 percent depending on the type of establishment is normal.

■ When ordering, it is common to say **dvakrát kávu** (literally 'a coffee, twice') rather than **dvě kávy** (two coffees).

■ Czechs consider it polite to say **Dobrou chuť!** (Enjoy your meal!) to their table companions before they start eating.

■ Prague offers a wealth of culinary experience and a wide range of restaurants in unique historical settings. For an evening meal in a popular restaurant, especially in the city centre, booking a table is essential.

You may see

Automat	Self-service cafeteria	**Rybí restaurant**	Fish restaurant
Bar	Bar	**Rychlé občerstvení**	Fast food
Bufet	Cafeteria, snack bar	**Jídelna (se samoobsluhou)**	(Self-service) cafeteria
Hospoda/ Hostinec	Pub/Tavern	**Šatna**	Cloakroom
Jídelní lístek	Menu	**Vinárna**	Wine bar
Kavárna	Coffee bar/Café	**Vinný sklípek**	Literally wine 'cellar', a wine bar with an interesting interior
Mléčný bar	Milk bar		
Muži	Men (toilets)		
Občerstvení	Refreshments	**WC**	Toilets
Pivnice	Beer hall/Pub	**Ženy**	Women (toilets)
Restaurace	Restaurant		

You may want to say

Are there any inexpensive restaurants near here?	**Jsou tu nějaké levnější restaurace?**	*ysoh tu nyeyakai levnyeyshee restauratse*
A ... please	**Jednou ... prosím**	*yednoh ... proseem*
Two of these, please	**Dvakrát tohle prosím**	*dvakraat tohle proseem*
Another one, please	**Ještě jednou prosím**	*yeshtye yednoh proseem*
For me/her/him	**Pro mě/ni/něho**	*pro mnye/nyi/nyeho*
This one, please	**Tohle prosím**	*tohle proseem*
Do you have ... ?	**Máte ... ?**	*maate*
Are there any ...?	**Máte nějaké ... ?**	*maate nyeyakai*
What is there for dessert?	**Jaké máte dezerty?**	*yakai maate dezerti*
What do you recommend?	**Co mi můžete doporučit?**	*tso mi moozhete doporuchit*

Do you have any typical Czech dishes?	Máte nějaká typická česká jídla?	*maate nyeyakaa típitskaa cheskaa yeedla*
What is this?	Co je tohle?	*tso ye tohle*
Cheers!	Na zdraví!	*na zdravee*
Enjoy your meal!	Dobrou chuť!	*dobroh khuty*
Nothing else, thanks	Děkuji, to bude vše	*dyekuyi to bude fshe*
The bill, please	Zaplatím prosím	*zaplatyeem proseem*
Where are the toilets?	Kde jsou záchody?	*gde ysoh zaakhodi*

In cafés and fast-food restaurants

A black coffee, please	Kávu prosím	*kaavu proseem*
With milk/cream	S mlékem/Se smetanou	*s mlaikem/se smetanoh*
Without milk	Bez mléka	*bez mlaika*
Two teas, please	Dvakrát čaj	*dvakraat chay*
A tea with milk/lemon	Čaj s mlékem/s citrónem	*chay s mlaikem/s tsitrawnem*
Mineral water, please	Minerálku prosím	*mineraalku proseem*
Fizzy/Still	Šumivou/Obyčejnou	*shumivoh/obicheynoh*
What fruit juices do you have?	Jaký máte džus?	*yakee maate dzhus*
An orange juice/A (small) beer, please	Pomerančový džus/(malé) Pivo prosím	*pomeranchovee dzhus/(malai) pivo proseem*
A glass of red/white wine, please	Sklenku červeného/bílého vína prosím	*sklenku chervenaiho/beelaiho veena proseem*
Dry/Medium dry/Sweet	Suché/Polosuché/Sladké	*sukhai/polosukhai/slatkai*
With ice	S ledem	*s ledem*
What ... do you have?	Jaké máte ...?	*yakai maate*
... (open) sandwiches	... chlebíčky	*khlebeechki*
... soups	... polévky	*polaifki*
A ham sandwich	Šunkový chlebíček	*shunkovee khlebeechek*
Two cheese sandwiches	Dva sýrové chlebíčky	*dva seerovai khlebeechki*

Two hot dogs	**Dvakrát párek v rohlíku**	*dvakrát paarek v rohleeku*
Do you have ice cream?	**Máte zmrzlinu?**	*maate zmrzlinu*
Chocolate/Vanilla	**Čokoládovou/ Vanilkovou**	*chokolaadovoh/ vanilkovoh*

Booking a table

I want to reserve a table for two	**Chtěl** (male)/**Chtěla** (female) **bych si zamluvit stůl pro dva**	*khtyel/khtyela bikh si zamluvit stool pro dva*
For eight o'clock	**Na osmou hodinu**	*na osmoh hodynu*
For tomorrow at half past six	**Zítra na půl sedmé**	*zeetra na pool sedmai*
I have reserved a table	**Mám rezervovaný stůl**	*maam rezervovanee stool*
The name is ...	**Na jméno ...**	*na ymaino*

In restaurants

A table for four, please	**Stůl pro čtyři prosím**	*stool pro chtirzhi proseem*
Outside/On the terrace ...	**Venku/Na terase ...**	*venku/na terase*
... if possible	**... pokud možno**	*pokut mozhno*
Waiter/waitress!	**Pane vrchní !**	*pane vrkhnyee*
The menu, please	**Jídelní lístek prosím**	*yeedelnyee leestek proseem*
Do you have a set menu?	**Máte nějaké menu?**	*maate nyeyakai menu*
Do you have vegetarian dishes?	**Máte jídla pro vegetariány?**	*maate yeedla pro vegetariaani*
The drinks list, please	**Nápojový lístek prosím**	*naapoyovee leestek proseem*
What starters do you have?	**Jaké máte předkrmy?**	*yakai maate przhetkrmi*
Does that come with vegetables?	**Je to se zeleninou?**	*ye to se zelenyinoh*
With chips/With a salad	**S hranolky/Se salátem**	*s hranolki/se salaatem*

77

With rice/With potatoes	S rýží/S brambory	s reezhee/s brambori
Does it cost extra?	Platí se za to zvlášť?	platyee se za to zvlaashty
For dessert ...	Jako dezert ...	yako dezert
A piece of ...	Kousek ...	kohsek
ice cream sundae ...	Zmrzlinový pohár ...	zmrzlinovee pohaar
... with whipped cream	... se šlehačkou	se shlehachkoh
... with chocolate	... s čokoládou	s chokolaadoh
... with fruit	... s ovocem	s ovotsem
ice cream	Zmrzlinu	zmrzlinu
... (chocolate)	... čokoládovou	chokolaadovoh
... (vanilla)	... vanilkovou	vanilkovoh
... (fruit)	... ovocnou	ovotsnoh
What cheeses are there?	Jaké sýry máte?	yakai seeri maate
More bread, please	Ještě chléb prosím	yeshtye khlaip proseem
A glass/jug of water	Sklenici/Džbánek vody	sklenyitsi/dzhbaanek vodi
A bottle/A glass of ...	Láhev/Sklenku ...	laahef/sklenku
... white/red wine	... bílého/červeného vína	beelaiho/chervenaiho veena
It's very good	Je to moc dobré	ye to mots dobrai
This is burnt	Je to připálené	ye to przhipaalenai
This is not cooked	Není to dovařené	nenyee to dovarzhenai
I didn't order this	To jsem si neobjednal (male)/neobjednala (female)	to ysem si neobyednal neobyednala
I ordered chicken	Objednal (male)/objednala (female) jsem si kuře	obyednal/obyednala ysem si kurzhe
The bill, please	Zaplatím prosím	zaplatyeem proseem
Do you accept credit cards?	Berete kreditní karty?	berete kreditnyee karti

Excuse me, there is a mistake here	**Promiňte, ale není to správně**	*prominyte ale nenyee to spraavnye*

You may hear

In cafés and fast food restaurants

Co si dáte?/Co to bude?	*tso si daate/tso to bude*	What will you have?
(Dáte si) něco k pití?	*daate si nyetso k pityee*	Would you like a drink?
Hned to bude	*hnet to bude*	Right away

In restaurants

Pro kolik lidí/osob?	*pro kolik lidyee/osop*	For how many people?
Máte rezervován stůl?	*maate rezervovaan stool*	Have you reserved a table?
Lituji, máme obsazeno	*lituyi maame opsazeno*	I'm sorry, we are full up
Počkáte si chvíli?	*pochkaate si khveeli*	Would you like to wait a while?
Máte vybráno?	*maate vibraano*	Have you made your choice yet?
(Co) k tomu (jako přílohu?)	*tso k tomu yako przheelohu*	What will you have with it?
... není/nejsou	*nenyee/neysoh*	There is/are no ...
Bude to všechno?	*bude to fshekhno*	Will that be all?
(Platíte) dohromady (nebo zvlášť?)	*platyeete dohromadi nebo zvlaashty*	(Would you like to pay) together (or separately)?

Menu reader

(See also EATING AND DRINKING, page 73)

General expressions and phrases

Alkoholické nápoje	Alcoholic beverages	**Nealkoholické nápoje**	Non-alcoholic drinks
Aperitivy	Aperitifs	**Oběd**	Lunch
Bezmasá jídla	Meatless dishes	**Polévky**	Soups
Ceník	Price list	**Porce**	Portion
Ceny včetně obsluhy	Service charge included	**Předkrmy**	Starters
Dezerty	Desserts	**... teplé**	... hot
Doporučujeme	We recommend	**... studené**	... cold
Drůbež	Poultry (dishes)	**Přílohy**	Side dishes
Hotová jídla	Ready made dishes	**Ryby**	Fish (dishes)
Jídelní lístek	Menu	**Saláty**	Salads
Jídla na objednávku	Dishes made to order	**Snídaně**	Breakfast
Krajové speciality	Local specialities	**Speciality šéfkuchaře**	Chef's specialities
Kuchyně	Cuisine	**Sýry**	Cheeses
Masitá jídla	Meat dishes	**Večeře**	Dinner
Minutky	Quick (meat) dishes to order	**Vegetariánská jídla**	Vegetarian dishes
Moučníky	Puddings	**Zvěřina**	Game
Nabídka dne	Dish(es) of the day		
Nápojový lístek	Drinks list		

Drinks

Alkoholické nápoje	Alcoholic beverages

Becherovka	Sweet herbal digestive liqueur
Bohemia sekt	Bohemian champagne
Borovička	Juniper-flavoured spirit
Budvar	Budweiser beer
Čaj (s citrónem/ mlékem)	Tea (with lemon/milk)
Destiláty	Spirits
Dobrá voda	Brand of mineral water (available both still and fizzy)
Džus	Juice
... grapefruitový	... grapefruit
... jablečný	... apple
... pomerančový	... orange
Fernet Stock	Bitter digestive liqueur
Gambrinus	Brand of beer
Grog	Hot drink made of dark rum, sugar and lemon
Káva	Coffee
... s mlékem	...with milk
... se šlehačkou	...with whipped cream
Turecká káva	Turkish (unfiltered) coffee
Káva kapucín	Cappuccino
(Es)preso	Espresso coffee
Vídeňská káva	Vienna coffee (with whipped cream)

Překapávaná káva	Filtered coffee
Instantní káva	Instant coffee
Irská káva	Irish coffee
Koktaily	Cocktails
Koňak	Cognac
Limonáda	Soft drink, not necessarily lemonade
Likéry	Liqueurs
Mattoni(ho kyselka)	Brand of sparkling mineral water
Minerálka	Mineral water
Myslivec (Stará myslivecká)	Czech brandy
Pivo	Beer
... černé/tmavé	... dark
... světlé	... light
... točené	... draught
... ležák	... lager
Plzeňské	Pilsner beer
Plzeňský prazdroj	Pilsner Urquell (brand of beer)
Sekt	Champagne
S ledem	With ice
Slivovice	Plum brandy
Staropramen	Brand of beer
Svařené víno	Mulled red wine
Tomatová štáva	Tomato juice
Vermut	Vermouth
Velkopopovický kozel	Brand of beer

Vína bílá	White wines
Vína červená	Red wines
Víno...	Wine
... suché	... dry
... polosuché	... medium dry
... sladké	... sweet

Food

Bavorské vdolky	Doughnuts with jam, soft cheese or cream
Bažant	Pheasant
Biftek s oblohou	Steak with garnish of pickled vegetables
Boršč	Beef and beetroot soup
Bramborák	Savoury potato pancake
Bramborová kaše	Mashed potatoes
Bramborový salát	Potato salad with mayonnaise
Brambory	Potatoes
... vařené	... boiled
... opékané	... roasted
Buchty	Buns filled with cottage cheese, jam or fruit
Bylinkové máslo	Herb butter
Chřest	Asparagus
Čevabčiči	Spicy meatballs

Čína	Chinese dish
Čočka	Lentils
Domácí	Home-made
Dort	Gateau/flan/cream cake
... čokoládový	Chocolate cake
... ořechový	Nut cake
Dušená rýže	Steamed rice
Dušený	Stewed/braised/ steamed
Grilovaný	Grilled
Guláš	Goulash (meat stew with paprika and onions)
Houby	(Wild) mushrooms
Hovězí	Beef
Hovězí biftek	Beef steak
Hovězí bujón	Beef bouillon
Hovězí vývar	Beef broth
.. s játrovými knelíčky	... with liver dumplings
... s nudlemi	... with noodles
Hranolky	Chips
Husa	Goose
Jablkový závin	Apple strudel
Játra	Liver
Jehněčí	Lamb
Jitrnice	Traditional cooked pork sausage made of offal
Kachna	Duck
... pečená	... roast
... s jablky	... with apples

... se zelím	... with pickled cabbage
Kapr	Carp
... pečený	... roast
... na rožni	... grilled
Karbenátky	Minced meat rissoles
Klobása	Sausage
Knedlíky	Dumplings
... bramborové	... made of boiled potato
... chlupaté	... made of raw potato
... houskové	bread ...
... kynuté	steamed ... made of yeast dough with sweet filling
... ovocné	... filled with fruit
Koláče	Pastry topped with fruit, jam or cottage cheese
Kotlet	Chop
... vepřový	... pork
... telecí	... veal
Králík	Rabbit
Krůta	Turkey
Kulajda	Potato and mushroom soup
Kuře	Chicken
Kuřecí	Chicken
... játra	... liver
....prsíčka	... breast
... stehna	... thighs

Květák	Cauliflower
... smažený	fried in bread crumbs/batter
Kyselé okurky	Pickled cucumbers
Kyselé zelí	Sour (pickled) cabbage
Lívance	Pancakes
... s marmeládou	... with jam
Lečo s klobásou	Stewed peppers and tomatoes with sausage and eggs
Moravští vrabci	Pieces of roast pork
Míchaná zelenina	Mixed vegetables
Na česneku	With garlic
Na houbách	With mushrooms
Na jehle	On a skewer
Na másle	Fried/braised in butter
Na paprice/ kmíně	With paprika/caraway
Na roštu	Grilled
Na smetaně	In cream sauce
Na víně	Cooked in wine
Niva	Czech blue cheese
Omáčka	Sauce
...koprová	... cream sauce with dill
...rajská	... thick tomato sauce
...houbová	... cream sauce with (wild) mushrooms

Omeleta	Omelette
... se žampióny	... with mushrooms
... s hráškem	... with peas
Palačinky	Pancakes/crêpes
... s ovocem	... with fruit
... s tvarohem	... with cottage cheese filling
Pečeně	Roast meat
Pečený	Roast (adj.)
Pečivo	Bread rolls
Pivní sýr	Cheese with a sharp taste
Plísňový sýr	Blue cheese
Polévka	Soup
... bramborová	... potato
... čočková	... lentil
... dršťková	... tripe
... gulášová	... goulash
... hovězí	... beef
... houbová	... mushroom
... rajská	... tomato
... zelná	... cabbage
Pražská šunka	Prague ham
Přírodní roštěná	Braised sirloin
Pstruh	Trout
... na másle	... fried in butter
... po mlynářsku	... coated in flour and fried
Restovaný	(Stir-)fried
Rostbíf	Roast beef
Rybí filé	Fillet of fish

Rýže	Rice
Rýžový nákyp	Rice pudding
Řízek	Pork schnitzel
S nádivkou	With stuffing
S oblohou	With garnish
Se šunkou	With ham
S vejcem	With an egg
Se zeleninou	With vegetables
Se zelím	With cabbage
Salám	Salami
Salát	Salad
... hlávkový	lettuce ...
... okurkový	cucumber ...
... rajčatový	tomato ...
... míchaný	mixed ...
... zelný	cabbage ...
Sardinky	Sardines
Sekaná	Meatloaf
Skopová kýta	Leg of mutton
Skopové	Mutton
Smažený	Fried in breadcrumbs or batter
Smažený řízek	(Pork/Veal) schnitzel
Smažený sýr	Cheese fried in breadcrumbs
Srnčí	Venison
... kýta na smetaně	leg of ... in cream sauce
... hřbet	saddle of ...
Studený nářez	Assorted cold meats and sausages

Svíčková na smetaně	Pot roasted fillet of beef with creamy vegetable sauce	... vařená	... boiled
		... ztracená	... poached
Šlehačka	Whipped cream	Vepřové	Pork
Španělské ptáčky	Stuffed beef olives	Vepřové žebírko	Pork rib
		Vepřový kotlet	Pork chop
Špenát	Spinach	Vepřový řízek	Pork schnitzel (fried in breadcrumbs)
Šunka s vejci	Ham and eggs		
Šunkový závitek	Sliced ham stuffed with savoury filling	Volské oko	Fried egg
		Zajíc	Hare
Švestkové knedlíky	Plum dumplings	... na divoko	... marinated and cooked with bacon, spices and wine
Tatarská omáčka	Tartar sauce		
Telecí	Veal	... na smetaně	... in cream sauce
Telecí řízek	Veal steak fried in breadcrumbs	Zavináče	Rollmop herrings
		Zelenina	Vegetables
Těstoviny	Pasta	Zelí	Cabbage
Tresčí játra	Cod liver	... bílé	... white
Tlačenka	Jellied meatloaf	... červené	... red
Tuňák	Tuna fish	... kyselé	... pickled
Uherský salám	Spicy salami	Zmrzlina	Ice cream
Utopenec	Pickled pork sausage	Zmrzlinový pohár	Ice cream sundae
Uzené maso	Smoked meat	... s ovocem	... with fruit
Uzený losos	Smoked salmon	... se šlehačkou	... with whipped cream
V těstíčku	Fried in batter		
Vařený	Boiled	Žampiony	Mushrooms
Vejce	Eggs	... plněné	... stuffed
... míchaná	... scrambled	... smažené	... fried in breadcrumbs
... ruská	... hard-boiled egg with mayonnaise		
... smažená	... fried		

Business trips

▌ (See also TELEPHONES, page 69)

▌ You'll probably be doing business with the help of interpreters or in a language everyone speaks, but you may need a few Czech phrases to cope at a company's reception desk.

▌ Titles are used with names more often than is usual in English, especially in work relationships. The title you are most likely to come across is **inženýr** (male)/**inženýrka** (female), used when addressing a person with a degree in civil, electrical or mechanical engineering and in economics and foreign trade. On a business card the abbreviation **ing.** will be used. The other frequently used title is **doktor** (male)/**doktorka** (female), even when the person is not a doctor of medicine (MUDr), but of other academic disciplines (PhDr – doctor of philosophy or arts, JUDr – doctor of law, RNDr – doctor of natural sciences, etc.). These people are referred to as **doktor Novák, inženýrka Kosová,** etc. but are addressed **pane doktore, paní inženýrko** etc.

▌ Note: remember that certain words take different endings depending on whether it's a man or a woman speaking (or being spoken about).

You may see

Firma	Firm	**Podnik**	Enterprise
Kouření zakázáno	No smoking	**Přízemí**	Ground floor
Mimo provoz	Out of order	**Společnost**	Company
Nepovolaným vstup zakázán	Entrance for authorised persons only	**S.r.o.**	Limited liability company
		Vchod	Entry
Nouzový východ	Emergency exit	**Východ**	Exit
... patro	... floor (storey)	**Výtah**	Lift

You may want to say

(See also DAYS, MONTHS, DATES, page 126, and TIME, page 124)

My name is ...	**Jmenuji se...**	*ymenuyi se*
I work for (the firm) ...	**Jsem z firmy ...**	*ysem s firmi*
I have an appointment with ...	**Mám schůzku s ...**	*maam skhoosku s*
I'd like to make an appointment ...	**Rád bych si dal** (male)/ **Ráda bych si dala** (female) **schůzku ...**	*raat bikh si dal/ raada bikh si dala skhoosku*
... with Mr Černý/Mrs Černá	**... s panem Černým/ paní Černou**	*s panem cherneem/ panyee chernoh*
... with ing. Novák	**... s inženýrem Novákem**	*s inzheneerem novaakem*
... with ing. Nováková	**... s inženýrkou Novákovou**	*s inzheneerkoh novaakovoh*
I'd like to talk to ...	**Rád bych mluvil** (male)/ **Ráda bych mluvila** (female) **s ...**	*raat bikh mluvil/ raada bikh mluvila s*
... the export/import manager	**... vedoucím exportu/ importu**	*vedohtseem eksportu/importu*
... the sales director	**... obchodním ředitelem**	*opkhodnyeem rzhedyitelem*
... the chief designer	**... hlavním projektantem**	*hlavnyeem proyek tantem*
Here's my card	**Tady je moje vizitka**	*tadi ye moye vizitka*
What is his/her name?	**Jak se jmenuje?**	*yak se ymenuye*
When will he/she be back?	**Kdy se vrátí?**	*gdi se vraatyee*
Can I leave a message?	**Můžu nechat vzkaz?**	*moozhu nekhat fskas*
Tell him to call me, please	**Řekněte mu** (him) **prosím, aby mi zavolal**	*rzheknyete mu proseem abi mi zavolal*

Tell her to call me, please	**Řekněte jí (her) prosím, aby zavolala mi**	*rzhek*nyete yee proseem *abi* mi zavolala
My telephone number is ...	**Moje telefonní číslo je ...**	*moye* tele*fonyee* *chees*lo ye
I'm staying at the Metropol Hotel	**Bydlím v hotelu Metropol**	*byd*leem v *ho*telu *met*ropol
Where is his/her office?	**Kde má kancelář?**	*gde* maa *kant*se laarzh
I'm here ...	**Jsem tu ...**	*ysem* tu
... for the conference/seminar	**... na konferenci/semináři**	*na* konferentsi/ seminaarzhi
I need to ...	**Potřebuji ...**	*potrzhe*buyi
... make a phone call (to England)	**... zavolat (do Anglie)**	zavolat *do* angliye
... send a telex/fax	**... poslat telex/fax**	poslat *teleks/faks*
... make a photocopy	**... udělat fotokopii**	udyelat *foto*kopiyi
Can you provide me with an interpreter?	**Můžete mi obstarat tlumočníka?**	*moo*zhete mi *op*starat *tlu*mochnyeeka?

You may hear

Jak se jmenujete prosím?	*yak* se *yme*nuyete proseem	What is your name, please?
Z jaké firmy jste?	z *yakai* *firmi* yste	Which firm do you work for?
Posaďte se prosím	*posatyte* se proseem	Please sit down
Počkejte okamžik	*pochkeyte* okamzhik	Please wait for a while
Pan ředitel má poradu	pan *rzhe*dyitel	The director
... má poradu	maa *poradu*	... is in a meeting
... je na služební cestě	ye *na* sluzhebnyee *tses*tye	... is away on business
... tu teď není	tu *tety* nenyee	... isn't in at the moment

Shopping

▌ Most shops are open from 8 or 9 a.m. to 5 or 6 p.m. Supermarkets and department stores have longer hours. Smaller shops often close for lunch. Most shops are open on Saturdays with the smaller ones closing at noon. On Sundays most shops are closed.

▌ Over-the-counter medicines can only be bought at a pharmacy (**Lékárna** or **Léky**). Stamps (**známky**) are sold at newsagents, kiosks with postcards, and post offices.

▌ A metric system is in use, so that prices for unpacked fruit and vegetables sold at the counter are given for kilograms. Prices for cold meats, delicatessen goods, etc. are indicated for 100 grams or kilograms, although customers normally use dekagrams (**deka**) as a unit (see also CONVERSION TABLES, page 133, and NUMBERS, page 121). The date of manufacture is often indicated on groceries rather than the use-by date.

▌ At the time of writing, credit cards are not widely accepted and can only be used in large department stores and tourist oriented shops in larger towns.

▌ If you wish to export anything of higher value the customs office (see USEFUL ADDRESSES, page 137), will give advice about duty-free limits and customs regulations, especially if you wish to export genuine antiques.

You may see

Types of shops

Antikvariát	Second-hand bookshop
Cukrárna	Cake/patisserie shop
Chemické čištění	Dry cleaning

Cukrovinky	Sweet shop
Dárky/Dárkové předměty	Gift shop
Domácí potřeby	Household goods shop
Drogerie	Chemist (without pharmacy)
Galanterie	Haberdashery
Hodiny/Hodinářství	Clock/watchmaker
Holičství	Hairdresser (men's)
Hračky/Hračkářství	Toy shop
Kadeřnictví	Hairdresser (women's)
Klenoty/Klenotnictví	Jeweller's
Knihy/Knihkupectví	Bookshop
Květiny/Květinářství	Flower shop
Lahůdky	Delicatessen
Lékárna/Léky	Pharmacy
Maso	Butcher
Mléčné lahůdky	Dairy delicacies shop
Mléčné výrobky	Dairy products
Nábytek	Furniture shop
Nákupní středisko	Shopping centre
Noviny-časopisy	Newsagent's
Obchodní dům	Department store
Obuv	Shoe shop
Oděvy (pánské/dámské)	Clothes (men's/women's) shop
Opravna obuvi	Shoe repairs
Optika	Optician
Ovoce-zelenina	Greengrocer
Papír/Papírnictví	Stationery
Partiové zboží	Imperfect goods
Parfumerie	Chemist (toiletries/cosmetics only)
Pečivo/Pekárna	Bakery
Pošta	Post office
Potraviny	Grocery
Ryby	Fishmonger
Samoobsluha	Self-service shop
Sklo-porcelán	Glass and china shop
Sportovní potřeby	Sports equipment shop
Stánek	Street kiosk
Starožitnosti	Antiques
Suvenýry	Souvenirs
Tabák/Trafika	Tobacconist
Tržnice	Market
Uzeniny	Cold meats, salamis and sausages
Večerka	Grocery with late opening hours

| Zlatnictví | Goldsmith |
| Železářství | Hardware shop |

Other signs and notices

Chléb – pečivo	Bread – pastries
Datum výroby	Date of manufacture
Doporučená spotřeba	Best before
Inventura	Closed for stocktaking
Otevřeno	Open
Otvírací hodiny	Opening hours
Pokladna	Cash desk
Přejímka zboží	Closed for deliveries
Spotřebujte do data uvedného na obalu	Consume by the date shown on the packaging
Výkup lahví	Empty bottles bought back here
Zavřeno	Closed

You may want to say

General phrases

(See also DIRECTIONS, page 33)

Where is the main shopping area?	**Kde je hlavní obchodní centrum?**	*gde ye hlavnyee opkhodnyee tsentrum*
Where is the pharmacy?	**Kde je lékárna?**	*gde ye laikaarna*
Is there a grocer's shop near here?	**Jsou tu blízko potraviny?**	*ysoh tu bleesko potravini*
Where can I buy batteries?	**Kde dostanu koupit baterie?**	*gde dostanu kohpit bateriye*
Where can I have my shoes repaired?	**Kde si můžu dát spravit boty?**	*gde si moozhu daat spravit boti*

What time ...?	**V kolik (hodin) ...?**	*f kolik (hodyin)*
... does the bakery open	**... se otvírá pečivo**	*se otveeraa pechivo*
... does the post office close	**... se zavírá pošta**	*se zaveeraa poshta*
... do you open in the morning	**... ráno otvíráte**	*raano otveeraate*
... do you close in the evening	**... večer zavíráte**	*vecher zaveeraate*
Do you have/Do you sell ... ?	**Máte .../Prodáváte ...?**	*maate/prodaavaate*
Can you show me ... ?	**Můžete mi ukázat ... ?**	*moozhete mi ukaazat*
How much is it?	**Kolik to stojí?**	*kolik to stoyee*
Altogether	**Dohromady**	*dohromadi*
I don't understand	**Nerozumím**	*nerozumeem*
Can you write it down, please?	**Napište mi to, prosím**	*napishte mi to proseem*
It's too expensive	**To je moc drahé**	*to ye mots drahai*
Have you got anything cheaper?	**Máte něco levnějšího?**	*maate nyetso levnyeysheeho*
I don't have enough money	**Nemám dost peněz**	*nemaam dost penyes*
Can you keep it for me?	**Můžete mi to rezervovat?**	*moozhete mi to rezervovat*
I'm just looking	**Jen se dívám**	*yen se dyeevaam*
This one, please	**Tohle prosím**	*tohle proseem*
That's fine	**To je dobré**	*to ye dobrai*
Nothing else, thank you	**To je vše, děkuji**	*to ye fshe dyekuyi*
I'll take it	**Vezmu si to**	*vezmu si to*
I'll think about it	**Rozmyslím si to**	*rozmysleem si to*
Can you wrap it, please?	**Můžete mi to zabalit prosím?**	*moozehete mi to zabalit proseem*
Where do I pay?	**Kde zaplatím?**	*gde zaplatyeem*
Do you take credit cards?	**Berete kreditní karty?**	*berete kreditnyee karti*

| I'm sorry, I don't have any change | **Bohužel nemám drobné** | *bohuzhel nemaam drobnai* |
| Can you give me a receipt, please? | **Dáte mi na to paragon prosím?** | *daate mi na to paragon proseem* |

Buying food and drink

(See also CONVERSION TABLES, page 133)

A kilo/Half a kilo of ...	**Kilo/půl kila ...**	*kilo/pool kila*
... grapes/apples/pears/ oranges/bananas/ tomatoes/peppers	**... hroznů/jablek/ hrušek/pomerančů/ banánů/rajčat/paprik**	*hroznoo/yablek/ hrushek/pomeranchoo/ banaanoo/raychat/ paprik*
Two hundred grams/A piece of ...	**Dvacet deka/Kousek ...**	*dvatset deka/kousek*
... salami/ham/cheese	**... salámu/šunky/sýra**	*salaamu/shunki/seera*
Sliced	**Krájený**	*kraayenee*
Two sausages	**Dvě klobásy**	*dvye klobaasi*
Two Frankfurters	**Dva párky**	*dva paarki*
Five slices of ham	**Pět plátků šunky**	*pyet plaatkoo shunki*
A bottle of red wine	**Lahev červeného vína**	*laahef chervenaiho veena*
A litre of water (sparkling/still)	**Litr vody (šumivé/nešumivé)**	*litr vodi shumivai/neshumivai*
Half a litre of milk	**Půl litru mléka**	*pool litru mlaika*
Two cans/bottles of beer	**Dvě plechovky/lahve piva**	*dvye plekhofki/laahve piva*
A bit of that, please	**Kousek tohohle prosím**	*kohsek tohohle proseem*
A bit more/less	**Trochu víc/míň**	*trokhu veets/meeny*
What is this?	**Co je tohle?**	*tso ye tohle*

Shopping

At the chemist

(See also HEALTH, page 106)

Aspirin/Paracetamol, please	**Aspirín/Paracetamol prosím**	*aspirin/paratsetamol proseem*
Plasters, please	**Náplast prosím**	*naaplast proseem*
Do you have something for diarrhoea?	**Máte něco proti průjmu?**	*maate nyetso protyi prooymu*
Do you have something for headaches?	**Máte něco proti bolení hlavy?**	*maate nyetso protyi bolenyee hlavi*

Buying clothes and shoes

I'm looking for ...	**Chtěl (male)/Chtěla (female) bych ...**	*khtyel/khtyela bikh*
... a dress/some sandals	**... nějaké šaty/sandály**	*nyeyakai shati/sandaali*
... a shirt/tie	**... nějakou košili/kravatu**	*nyeyakoh koshili/kravatu*
I'm size 40	**Mám čtyřicítku velikost**	*maam chtirzhitseetku velikost*
Can I try it on?	**Můžu si to zkusit?**	*moozhu si to skusit*
I like it	**Líbí se mi to**	*leebee se mi to*
I don't like it	**Nelíbí se mi to**	*neleebee se mi to*
Do you have it in other colours?	**Máte to v jiných barvách?**	*maate to v yineekh barvaakh*
It's too big/small	**Je to moc velké/malé**	*ye to mots velkai/malai*
Have you got a smaller/ bigger size?	**Máte to v menším/ větším čísle?**	*maate to v mensheem/ vyetsheem cheesle*

Miscellaneous

Five stamps for England, please	**Pět známek do Anglie**	*pyet znaamek do angliye*
Three postcards	**Tři pohledy**	*trzhi pohledi*
A packet of cigarettes	**krabičku cigaret**	*krabichku tsigaret*

94

Matches	Zápalky	*zaapalki*
A film for this camera	Film do tohoto aparátu	*film do tohoto aparaatu*
Do you have any English/American newspapers?	Máte nějaké anglické/ americké noviny?	*maate nyeyakai anglitskai/ameritskai novini*

You may hear

Další prosím	*dalshee proseem*	Who's next?
Prosím	*proseem*	What can I do for you?
Máte přání?/Přejete si?	*maate przhaanyee/ przheyete si*	How can I help you?
Bohužel, už nemáme/ to neprodáváme	*bohuzhel uzh nemaame to neprodaavaame*	Sorry, we're out of stock/ we don't sell that
Bude to všechno?	*bude to fshekhno*	Will that be all?
Ještě něco?/Další přání?	*yeshtye nyetso/dalshee przhaanyee*	Anything else?
Kolik chcete?	*kolik khtsete*	How much do you want?
Krájený nebo vcelku?	*kraayenee nebo ftselku*	Sliced or in one piece?
Jakou velikost?	*yakoh velikost*	What size?
Je to dobré?	*ye to dobrai*	Is that all right?
Nemáte něco menšího?	*nemaate nyetso mensheeho*	Do you have any smaller notes?

■ Information and English-language leaflets and brochures about the sights worth seeing can be obtained at the Czech Tourist Centre (**České turistické centrum**), and the **Čedok** travel agency (see USEFUL ADDRESSES, page 137) which also offers tours and excursions, and local tourist information offices. The Prague Information Service (**Pražská informační služba – PIS**) provides information about the sights and entertainment in the capital city.

■ A quick way to see Prague's major sights is to take one of the guided sightseeing tours organised by many agencies, or you can do it yourself in a cheaper way on board the special historic No.91 tram which runs from Easter to the end of October.

■ Museums, galleries and most sights in Prague and other major cities are open daily except Mondays all year round. Some gardens, however, are only open from spring to early autumn. Chateaux, castles and other historical monuments outside major cities are normally open from April to the end of September.

You may see

Kouření zakázáno	No smoking
Nedotýkat se	Do not touch
Nevstupujte na trávníky	Keep off the grass
Okružní jízda s průvodcem	Guided round trip
Otevřeno	Open
Otvírací/Návštěvní hodiny	Opening/Visiting hours
Pokladna	Ticket office
Prohlídky s průvodcem	Guided tours
Prohlídky s anglickým výkladem	Tours with English commentary
Stálá expozice	Permanent exhibition

Vstup pouze pro zaměstnance	Entry for staff only	
Vstupné	Admission	
... Dospělí	... Adults	
... Děti	... Children	
... Studenti/důchodci	... Students/OAPs	
Vstup zdarma	Admission free	
Výlety s průvodcem	Guided excursions	
Zavřeno	Closed	

You may want to say

(See also AT THE TOURIST OFFICE, page 61)

Opening times

(See also TIME, page 124)

When/What time ...?	**Kdy/V kolik hodin ...?**	*gdi/fkolik hodyin*
... is the museum open	**... se otvírá muzeum**	*se otveeraa muzeum*
... does the palace close	**... se zavírá ten palác**	*se zaveeraa ten palaats*
Is it open on Sundays?	**Je otevřeno o nedělích?**	*ye otevrzheno o nedyeleekh*

Visiting places

One/Two tickets, please	**Jednu/Dvě vstupenky prosím**	*yednu/dvye fstupenki proseem*
One adult/Two adults	**Jeden dospělý/Dva dospělí**	*yeden dospyelee/dva dospyelee*
... and one child/two children	**... a jedno dítě/dvě děti**	*a yedno dyeetye/dvye dyetyi*
For students/pensioners/ groups	**Pro studenty/důchodce/ skupiny**	*pro studenti/dookhotse/ skupini*

Are there guided tours/ trips?	**Pořádají se prohlídky/ výlety s průvodcem?**	*porzhaadayee se prohleetki/veeleti s proovotsem*
Can I/we take photos?	**Smí se tu fotografovat?**	*smee se tu fotografovat*
When was this built?	**Kdy to bylo postaveno?**	*gdi to bilo postaveno*
Who painted that picture?	**Kdo ten obraz namaloval?**	*gdo ten obras namaloval*
When?	**Kdy?**	*gdi*
Who lived in this place?	**Kdo tu žil?**	*gdo tu zhil*
Do you have a guide/ leaflets in English?	**Máte průvodce/ prospekty v angličtině?**	*maate proovotse/ prospekti f anglichtinye*
What time is mass?	**Kdy začíná mše?**	*gdi zacheenaa mshe*

Sightseeing excursions

Are there any trips to Karlštejn?	**Pořádají se výlety na Karlštejn?**	*porzhaadayee se veeleti na karlshteyn*
What time do I/we have to be there?	**V kolik tam musím/ musíme být?**	*fkolik tam museem/ museeme beet*
What time do we get back?	**V kolik se vrátíme?**	*fkolik se vraatyeeme*
Does the guide speak English?	**Mluví průvodce anglicky?**	*mluvee proovotse anglitski*
How much is it?	**Kolik to stojí?**	*kolik to stoyee*

You may hear

Prohlídky jsou denně kromě pondělků	*prohleetki soh denye kromye pondyelkoo*	Tours take place daily except Mondays
Autokar odjíždí ...	*autokar otyeezhdyee*	The coach leaves ...
... v deset hodin	*v deset hodyin*	... at ten o'clock
... z náměstí Republiky	*z naamyestyee republiki*	... from Republic Square

▌ The Czech Republic offers excellent opportunities for hiking along a network of well-marked scenic trails. A considerable part of the country is covered by dense forests, probably the most unspoilt being found in South Bohemia (the Šumava national park). Rock climbing is popular in northern and eastern Bohemia (e.g. České Švýcarsko and Český ráj). Several rivers (the Sázava in Central Bohemia and the upper flow of the Vltava in South Bohemia) offer opportunities for canoeing and kayaking. Water sports, such as windsurfing and water skiing, on the country's lakes (Lipno in South Bohemia and Vranov in South Moravia) are catching on quickly, although it may not be easy to hire equipment. In winter, skiing is very popular, mainly in the Krkonoše mountains, the Czech Republic's highest range.

▌ Licences for fishing can be obtained through travel agencies. Tennis courts are available in all larger towns and the number of golf courses is increasing with the growing popularity of the sport.

▌ There are more than two dozen spa towns concentrated mainly in West Bohemia, where ailments ranging from digestive to respiratory problems are treated.

▌ In Prague, there are opportunities for swimming, tennis, golf, cycling and rowing, and even horse riding. The woods just outside the capital provide a scenic backdrop for hiking. The Prague Information Service PIS (see USEFUL ADDRESSES, page 137) has information on outdoor and indoor sporting opportunities.

You may see

Bazén	Swimming pool
Bazén s ohřívanou vodou	Heated swimming pool
Dostihová dráha	Race course

Dostihy	Horse racing
Koupaliště	Outdoor swimming pool
Koupání zakázáno	No bathing/swimming
Krytý plavecký bazén	Indoor swimming pool
Lanovka	Cable car
Lyžařský vlek	Ski lift
Nebezpečí (lavin)	Danger (of avalanches)
Půjčovna lodí	Boat hire
Půjčovna lyží	Ski hire
Půjčovna sportovních potřeb	Sports equipment hire
Sedačková lanovka	Chair lift
Turistická stezka	Tourist path
Zákaz koupání	No bathing/swimming
Zákaz rybaření	No fishing

You may want to say

Is it possible to ...?	Je možné ...?	ye mozhnai
... do cycle tours here	... tu dělat výlety na kole	tu dyelat veeleti na kole
... go fishing	... jít na ryby	yeet na ribi
... go horse riding	... jezdit na koni	yezdyit na konyi
Where can we ...?	Kde si můžeme ...?	gde si moozheme
... play tennis	... zahrát tenis	zahraat tenis
... play golf	... zahrát golf	zahraat golf
Where can we go climbing?	Kde se dají dělat horolezecké túry?	gde se dayee dyelat horolezetskai toori
I don't know how to ...	Neumím ...	neumeem
I can ... (a bit/well)	Umím (trochu/dobře) ...	umeem trokhu/dobrzhe
... row ...	... veslovat ...	veslovat
... ski ...	... lyžovat ...	lizhovat
... swim ...	... plavat ...	plavat

... play tennis ...	... hrát tenis ...	*hraat tenis*
I am a beginner	Jsem začátečník	*ysem zachaatechnyeek*
Do you give lessons?	Dáváte lekce?	*daavaate lektse*
How much is it ...?	Kolik to stojí ...?	*kolik to stoyee*
... per hour/per day	... na hodinu/na den	*na hodyinu/na den*
Is there a reduction for children?	Mají děti slevu?	*mayee dyetyi slevu*
Can I/we hire ...?	Můžu/Můžeme si vypůjčit ...?	*moozhu/moozheme si vipoochit*
... bicycles/rackets/golf clubs/skis?	... kola/rakety/golfové hole/lyže?	*kola/raketi/golfovai hole/lizhe*
Is it necessary to be a member?	Je nutné být členem?	*ye nutnai beet chlenem*
Can I/we swim here?	Dá se tu plavat?	*daa se tu plavat*
Is it dangerous?	Je to nebezpečné?	*ye to nebespechnai*
How deep is the water here?	Jak je tu hluboko?	*yak ye tu hluboko*
Is there a ski run for beginners?	Je tu lyžařská sjezdovka pro začátečníky?	*ye tu lizharzhskaa syezdofka pro zachaatechnyeeki*
How much is the lift pass?	Kolik stojí permanentka na vlek?	*kolik stoyee permanentka na vlek*
Per day	Na den	*na den*
Per week	Na týden	*na teeden*
What time is the last ascent?	Kdy je poslední jízda nahoru?	*gdi ye poslednyee yeezda nahoru*

You may hear

Jste začátečník (male)/ začátečnice (female)?	*yste zachaatechnyeek/ zachaatechnyitse*	Are you a beginner?
Umíte veslovat/ jezdit na koni?	*umeete veslovat/ yezdyit na konyi*	Do you know how to row/ ride?
Přijďte prosím později	*przhityte proseem pozdyeyi*	Please come back later

101

Entertainment

■ There is a wide variety of entertainment opportunities in the capital, Prague, ranging from classical music, opera and ballet to first-class jazz music, rock, musicals and theatre. Cinemas keep up-to-date with Western premières shown either dubbed or with subtitles. Prague also boasts a tradition in mime and puppet theatre, and it is the home of an internationally acclaimed multi-media theatre, Laterna Magica.

■ Tickets are available through travel agencies and ticket agencies or directly at the box office. As a last resort, you can still try your luck for returned tickets at the box office half an hour before the performance.

■ The Prague Information Service (PIS) and English language weeklies published in Prague provide listings and information in English.

■ In the summer months, when most theatres and operas are closed for the holidays, some churches, chateaux and other historical monuments become concert venues. There are theatre companies and music ensembles in all larger towns.

■ The most popular spectator sports are football (soccer), ice-hockey, and tennis. Prague's main racecourse is at Velká Chuchle, but the country's best steeplechase is at Pardubice, east of the capital.

You may see

Balkón	Balcony	**Dnešní/Příští program**	Now showing/Coming soon
Diskotéka	Discotheque	**Dostihy**	Horse Racing
Divadlo	Theatre	**Hlavní tribuna**	Grandstand

Kino	Cinema
Lístky na dnešní představení	Tickets for tonight's performance
K stání	Standing places
Koncertní síň	Concert hall
Křesla	Stalls
Lóže	Boxes
Občerstvení	Refreshments
Odpolední představení	Matinée
Opera	Opera house
Po začátku představení není dovolen přístup do hlediště	No entry to the auditorium once performance has begun
Premiéra	Première
Program	Programme
První/Druhé pořadí	Dress/Upper Circle
První řada	Orchestra stalls
Předprodej	Advance booking
Představení	Performance
Přestávka	Interval
Přestávka po 1. jednání	Interval after the first act
Řada	Row
Stadion	Stadium
Šatny	Cloakrooms
Taneční sál	Dance hall
Večerní představení	Evening performance
Vlevo	Left
Vpravo	Right
Vstupenka	Ticket
Vyprodáno	Sold out

You may want to say

What is on

What is on tonight/tomorrow?	Co se hraje dnes večer/zítra?	*tso* se *hraye* dnes *vecher/zeetra*
At the cinema/At the theatre	V kině/V divadle	f *kinye*/v *dyivadle*
Where is the ... being shown?	Kde se hraje ... ?	*gde* se *hraye*
... musical ...	... ten muzikál	ten *muzikaal*
... new film ...	... ten nový film	ten *novee* *film*

103

Is there a disco near here?	Je tu blízko nějaká diskotéka?	*ye tu bleesko nyeyakaa diskotaika*
Does the film have subtitles?	Je ten film s titulky?	*ye ten film s titulki*
Where can I/we get tickets?	Kde se dají koupit lístky?	*gde se dayee kohpit leestki*
Who is playing?	Kdo hraje?	*gdo hraye*
When does it start/end?	Kdy to začíná/končí?	*gdi to zacheenaa/ konchee*

Tickets

Can you get me tickets for ...?	Můžete mi obstarat lístky na ...?	*moozhete mi opstarat leestki na*
... a ballet/an opera/a concert/football match	balet/operu/koncert/ fotbal	*balet/operu/kontsert/ fodbal*
Two for ...	Dva na ...	*dva na*
... tonight	... dnes večer	*dnes vecher*
... tomorrow night	... zítra večer	*zítra vecher*
... Friday	... pátek	*paatek*
Two for the 11 o'clock screening, please	Dva na jedenáctou (hodinu) prosím	*dva na yedenaatstoh (hodyinu) proseem*
Are there any seats left for ...?	Máte ještě lístky na ... ?	*maate yeshtye leestki na*
... Saturday	... sobotu	*sobotu*
... the afternoon showing	... odpoledne	*otpoledne*
... the 8 o'clock	... osmou hodinu	*osmoh hodyinu*
A box for four, please	Lóži pro čtyři prosím	*lawzhi pro chtyrzhi proseem*
Somewhere in the front/ middle	Někde vpředu/ uprostřed	*nyegde fprzhedu/ uprostrzhet*
Not too far back	Ne moc vzadu	*ne mots vzadu*
Tenth row/In the middle	Desátou řadu/ Uprostřed	*desaatoh rzhadu/ uprostrzhet*
How much is it?	Kolik to stojí?	*kolik to stoyee*
Do you have any	Máte něco	*maate nyetso*

cheaper?	**levnějšího?**	*levnyeysheeho*

At the show/game

Where is this seat, please?	**Kde je tohle místo prosím?**	*gde ye tohle **mee**sto proseem*
Where can I/we get a programme?	**Kde dostanu program?**	*gde dostanu **pro**gram*
Where is the cloakroom?	**Kde jsou šatny?**	*gde ysoh **shat**ni*
Where are the toilets?	**Kde jsou záchody?**	*gde ysoh **zaa**khodi*
Is there an interval?	**Bude přestávka?**	*bude przhe**staa**fka*

You may hear

Na kdy chcete vstupenky?	*na gdi khtsete **fstu**penki*	When would you like the tickets for?
Do které řady?	*do kterai **rzha**di*	Which row would you like?
Začátek je v sedm hodin	*za**chaa**tek ye f **sedm** hodyin*	It begins at seven o'clock
Trvá to dvě a půl hodiny	*trvaa to **dvye** a pool **ho**dyini*	It lasts two and a half hours
Končí to v půl desáté	*konchee to f **pool** de**saa**tai*	It ends at half past nine
Bude patnáctiminutová přestávka	*bude pat**naatsty**i- minutovaa przhe**staa**fka*	There is a 15-minute interval
Křesla nebo první pořadí?	*krzhesla nebo **prv**nyee **po**rzhadyee*	In the stalls or in the circle?
Je vyprodáno	*ye vi**pro**daano*	We're sold out
Máme jen balkón	*maame yen **bal**kawn*	There is only the balcony left
Vstupenky prosím	*fstupenki proseem*	Your tickets, please

105

(See also EMERGENCIES, page 119, and USEFUL AND EMERGENCY
TELEPHONE NUMBERS, page 139)

▌ Emergency treatment is provided free of charge to all foreigners.
You will need to show your passport. In an emergency call an
ambulance (**Záchranná služba**) or visit a first-aid centre (**Lékařská
služba první pomoci**). You will find the address of the nearest
centre in the telephone directory.

▌ All other non-essential treatment must be paid for. A receipt is
needed for insurance purposes. However, for British visitors,
medical assistance is free of charge under a reciprocal health-care
agreement between the two countries.

▌ You can consult a doctor at a local polyclinic (**poliklinika**). There
are polyclinics in every larger town and in every Prague borough. If
you need immediate help, polyclinics have after-hours emergency
services (**pohotovost**). Some Czech will be useful, especially
outside larger cities. In Prague, there is a special health centre for
foreigners (**Nemocnice Na Homolce**), including a dental clinic, and
a centrally situated polyclinic (**Fakultní poliklinika**) where you can
see an English-speaking doctor.

▌ There are 24-hour pharmacies (**lékárna**) whose addresses will be
displayed on the door of a local pharmacy and are listed in the
telephone directory.

Medical details – to show to a doctor

(Tick where appropriate or fill in details)		Self	Other members of the family/party
		Já	**Jiní členové rodiny/skupiny**
Blood group	**Krevní skupina**		
Asthmatic	**Astmatik**		
Blind	**Slepý**		

Deaf	**Hluchý**
Diabetic	**Diabetik**
Epileptic	**Epileptik**
Handicapped	**Tělesně postižený**
Heart condition	**Srdeční choroba**
High blood pressure	**Vysoký krevní tlak**
Pregnant	**Těhotná**
Allergic to ...	**Alergie na ...**
Antibiotics	**Antibiotika**
Penicillin	**Penicilín**
Cortisone	**Kortizon**
Medicines	**Léky**

You may see

Ambulantní služba	Outpatients surgery
Jed	Poison
Jen k zevnímu použítí	For external use only
Kapky	Drops
Lékárna	Pharmacy
Lékař	Doctor
Lékařská služba první pomoci	First aid service
Použití	How to take/Directions
Dvakrát 2 tablety denně	Two tablets twice a day
Každé 4 hodiny	Every four hours
Před jídlem/Po jídle	Before meals/After meals
Nepodávat dětem do 12 let	Not to be given to children under 12 years
Nemocnice	Hospital
Ordinace	Surgery
Ordinační hodiny	Surgery hours

Pohotovost	Emergency duty
Poliklinika	Polyclinic
Prodej za hotové	Over-the-counter medicines
Před použitím protřepat	Shake before use
Výdej na recepty	Prescription counter
Zubní středisko	Dentist

You may want to say

At the surgery

I need a doctor	**Potřebuji doktora**	*potrzhebuyi doktora*
Quickly	**Rychle**	*rikhle*
Is there someone who speaks English?	**Mluví někdo anglicky?**	*mluvee nyegdo anglitski*
Can I make an appointment?	**Můžu se objednat?**	*moozhu se obyednat*
It's my ...	**Jde o ...**	*yde o*
... husband/son wife/daughter/ friend	**...manžela/syna/ manželku/dceru/ známého** (male)/ **známou** (female)	*manzhela/sina/ manzhelku/tseru/ znaamaiho/znaamoh*
How much will it cost?	**Kolik to bude stát?**	*kolik to bude staat*

Your symptoms

I feel unwell	**Necítím se dobře**	*netseetyeem se dobrzhe*
It hurts here	**Tady mě bolí**	*tadi mnye bolee*
My ... hurts/hurt	**Bolí mě ...**	*bolee mnye*
My eyes/stomach/back hurt(s)	**Bolí mě oči/břicho/záda**	*bolee mnye ochi/brzhikho/zaada*
I have a sore throat	**Bolí mě v krku**	*bolee mnye f krku*
I have a toothache	**Bolí mě zub**	*bolee mnye zup*

I have a temperature	**Mám teplotu**	*maam teplotu*
I have diarrhoea	**Mám průjem**	*maam prooyem*
I feel dizzy	**Točí se mi hlava**	*tochee se mi hlava*
I feel sick	**Je mi nevolno**	*ye mi nevolno*
I have been sick	**Zvracel jsem** (male) **Zvracela jsem** (female)	*zvratsel ysem/zvratsela ysem*
I can't sleep	**Nemůžu spát**	*nemoozhu spaat*
I can't breathe	**Nemůžu dýchat**	*nemoozhu deekhat*
I can't move my ...	**Nemůžu hýbat ...**	*nemoozhu heebat*
... finger/hand/head	**... prstem/rukou/hlavou**	*prstem/rukoh/hlavoh*
I'm bleeding	**Krvácím**	*krvaatseem*
It's my arm/leg/ankle	**Mám něco s rukou/ nohou/kotníkem**	*maam nyetso s rukoh/ nohoh/kotnyeekem*
I think that ...	**Myslím, že ...**	*misleem zhe*
... it's broken	**... je to zlomenina**	*ye to zlomenyina*
... it's sprained	**... je to výron**	*ye to veeron*
I have cut myself	**Pořezal** (male)/ **Pořezala** (female) **jsem se**	*porzhezal/porzhezala ysem se*
I have burnt myself	**Popálil** (male)/**Popálila** (female) **jsem se**	*popaalil/popaalila ysem se*
I have been stung by a bee/wasp	**Bodla mě včela/vosa**	*bodla mnye fchela/ vosa*
I have been bitten by a dog	**Pokousal mě pes**	*pokohsal mnye pes*

Someone else's symptoms

He/She feels unwell	**Necítí se dobře**	*netseetyee se dobrzhe*
He/She is unconscious	**Je v bezvědomí**	*ye v bezvyedomee*
It hurts here	**Tady ho** (male)/ **ji** (female) **bolí**	*tadi ho/yi bolee*
His/Her stomach/back/eyes/ feet hurt(s)	**Bolí ho** (male)/**ji** (female) **břicho/záda/ oči/chodidla**	*bolee ho/yi brzhikho/ zaada/ochi/khodyidla*

He/She has a sore throat	Bolí ho (male)/ji (female) v krku	*bolee ho/yi f krku*
He/She has a temperature	Má teplotu	*maa teplotu*
He/She feels dizzy	Točí se mu (male)/ jí (female) hlava	*tochee se mu/yee hlava*
He/She feels sick	Je mu (male)/jí (female) nevolno	*ye mu/yee nevolno*
He/She has been sick	Zvracel (male)/ Zvracela (female)	*zvratsel/zvratsela*
He/She is bleeding	Krvácí	*krvaatsee*
It's his/her ...	Má něco s ...	*maa nyetso s*
... ankle/leg/arm/wrist	... kotníkem/nohou/ rukou/zápěstím	*kotnyeekem/nohoh/ rukoh/zaapyestyeem*
He/She has cut himself/ herself	Pořezal (male)/Pořezala (female) se	*porzhezal/porzhezala se*
He/She has burnt himself/ herself	Popálil (male)/Popálila (female) se	*popaalil/popaalila se*
He/She has been stung by an insect	Bodnul ho (male)/ ji (female) hmyz	*bodnul ho/yi hmis*
He/She has been bitten by a dog	Pokousal ho (male)/ji (female) pes	*pokohsal ho/yi pes*

You may hear

Co se stalo?	*tso se stalo*	What happened?
Kde vás bolí?	*gde vaas bolee*	Where does it hurt?
Svlékněte se prosím	*svlaiknyete se proseem*	Please get undressed
Není to nic vážného	*nenyee to nyits vaazhnaiho*	It's nothing serious
Který zub to je ?	*kteree zup to ye*	Which tooth is it?

ankle	**kotník**	*kotnyeek*
appendix	**apendix**	*apendiks*
arm	**ruka**	*ruka*
back	**záda**	*zaada*
bladder	**močový měchýř**	*mochovee mnyekheerzh*
blood	**krev**	*kref*
body	**tělo**	*tyelo*
bone	**kost**	*kost*
bottom	**hýždě/zadek** (colloquial)	*heezhdye/zadek*
bowels	**střeva**	*strzheva*
breast	**prs**	*prs*
buttock	**hýždě**	*heezhdye*
cartilage	**chrupavka**	*khrupafka*
chest	**hrudník**	*hrudnyeek*
chin	**brada**	*brada*
ear	**ucho**	*ukho*
eye	**oko**	*oko*
face	**obličej**	*oblichey*
finger	**prst**	*prst*
foot	**chodidlo**	*khodyidlo*
genitals	**genitálie**	*genitaaliye*
gland	**žláza**	*zhlaaza*
hair	**vlasy**	*vlasi*
hand	**ruka**	*ruka*
head	**hlava**	*hlava*
heart	**srdce**	*srtse*
heel	**pata**	*pata*
hip	**kyčel**	*kichel*
jaw	**čelist**	*chelist*
joint	**kloub**	*klohp*

kidney	ledviny	ledvini
knee	koleno	koleno
leg	noha	noha
ligament	vazivo	vazivo
lip	ret	ret
liver	játra	yaatra
lung	plíce	pleetse
mouth	ústa	oosta
muscle	sval	sval
nail	nehet	nehet
neck	krk	krk
nerve	nerv	nerf
nose	nos	nos
penis	penis	penis
rectum	konečník	konechnyeek
rib	žebro	zhebro
shoulder	rameno	rameno
skin	kůže	koozhe
spine	páteř	paaterzh
stomach	břicho/žaludek (the organ)	brzhikho/zhaludek
tendon	šlacha	shlakha
testicles	varlata	varlata
thigh	stehno	stehno
throat	krk	krk
thumb	palec	palets
toe	prst u nohy	prst u nohi
tongue	jazyk	yazik
tonsils	krční mandle	krchnyee mandle
tooth	zub	zup
vagina	vagína	vageena
wrist	zápěstí	zaapyestyee

Problems and complaints

▌ (For car breakdowns, see ROAD TRAVEL, page 36, for health problems see HEALTH, page 106. See also EMERGENCIES, page 119)

▌ There are two main types of police force in the Czech Republic, both armed: the **policie České republiky** (state police) controlled by the Ministry of the Interior and the **městská policie** (municipal police) run by the local authorities. The municipal police are in charge of maintaining law and order and are further divided into several sections.

▌ Road accidents are dealt with by the **dopravní policie** (traffic police) and serious crime by the **kriminální policie** (criminal police). There is also a number of private security agencies.

▌ You can go either to the nearest police station or the main police station in the town where you are staying. Your hotel management may put you in touch with one. Since English is not usually spoken, your embassy in Prague (see USEFUL ADDRESSES, page 137) may be the first port of call.

▌ A lost or stolen passport should be reported to your embassy in Prague and to the foreigners' police and passport office (**Cizinecká policie a pasová služba**; see USEFUL ADDRESSES, page 137) in Prague and all regional capitals, which will issue a replacement visa. You are expected to carry some form of ID at all times.

You may see

Hasičská stanice	Fire brigade
Kniha přání a stížností	Book of suggestions and complaints
Lékařská služba první pomoci	First aid service
Mimo provoz	Out of order

Pohotovostní služba	Emergencies
Policie	Police
Zavřeno	Closed
Ztráty a nálezy	Lost property office
Z technických důvodů zavřeno	Closed for technical reasons

You may want to say

General phrases

I need ...	Potřebuji ...	**po**trzhebuyi
I need help	Potřebuji pomoc	**po**trzhebuyi **po**mots
Can you fix it (immediately)?	Můžete to (hned) opravit?	**moo**zhete to (**hnet**) **o**pravit
When can you fix it?	Kdy to můžete opravit?	**gdi** to **moo**zhete **o**pravit
Can I speak to the manager?	Můžu mluvit s vedoucím?	**moo**zhu mluvit s **ve**dohtseem
The problem is ...	Problém je, že ...	**prob**laim ye zhe
There isn't/aren't any ...	Není tu/Nejsou tu ...	**ne**nyee tu/**ney**soh tu
It doesn't work	Nefunguje to	**ne**funguye to
It's broken	Je to pokažené	ye to **po**kazhenai
... is missing	Chybí tu ...	**khi**bee tu
I can't ...	Nemůžu ...	**ne**moozhu
It wasn't my fault	Nemůžu za to ...	**ne**moozhu **za** to
I've forgotten my ...	Zapomněl (male)/ Zapomněla(female) jsem ...	**za**pomnyel/**za**pomnyela ysem
I've lost my ...	Ztratil (male)/ Ztratila (female) jsem ...	**stray**tyil/**stra**tyila ysem
We've lost our ...	Ztratili jsme...	**stra**tyili ysme
Someone has stolen my ...	Někdo mi ukradl ...	**nyeg**do mi ukradl

114

I've just been robbed	**Právě mě okradli**	*praavye mye okradli*
It has disappeared	**Zmizelo to**	*zmizelo to*
It is missing	**Ztratilo se to**	*stratyilo se to*
This isn't mine	**To není moje**	*to nenyee moye*

Where you're staying

There isn't/aren't any ...	**Chybí tu ...**	*khibee tu*
... toilet paper	**... toaletní papír**	*toaletnye papeer*
... towels	**... ručníky**	*ruchnyeeki*
... blankets	**... přikrývky**	*przhikreefki*
I need ...	**Potřebuji ...**	*potrzhebuyi*
... another blanket	**... ještě jednu přikrývku**	*yeshtye yednu przhikreefku*
... another pillow	**... ještě jeden polštář**	*yeshtye yeden polshtaarzh*
... a light bulb	**... novou žárovku**	*novoh zhaarofku*
There isn't any hot water	**Neteče teplá voda**	*neteche teplaa voda*
There isn't any electricity	**Nejde proud**	*neyde proht*
The shower/light/lock/switch/TV/heating doesn't work	**Sprcha/světlo/zámek/vypínač/televize/topení nefunguje**	*sprkha/svyetlo/zaamek/vipeenach/televize/topenyee nefunguye*
I can't ...	**Nemůžu ...**	*nemoozhu*
... open/shut the window/door	**... otevřít/zavřít okno/dveře**	*otevrzheet/zavrzheet okno/dverzhe*
... flush the toilet	**... splachovat**	*splakhovat*
... switch on the light	**... rozsvítit světlo**	*rosveetyit svyetlo*
The washbasin is ...	**Umyvadlo je ...**	*umivadlo ye*
... blocked/dirty	**... ucpané/špinavé**	*utspanai/shpinavai*
It's very noisy	**Je tu velký hluk**	*ye tu velkee hluk*
There's a smell of gas	**Je cítit plyn**	*ye tseetyit plin*

In bars and restaurants

This isn't cooked	**Je to syrové**	*ye to sirovai*
This is burnt/cold	**Je to spálené/studené**	*ye to spaalenai/ studenai*
I didn't order this	**Tohle jsem si neobjednal** (male)/ **neobjednala** (female)	*tohle ysem si neobyednal/ neobyednala*
I wanted ...	**Chtěl/chtěla jsem ...**	*khtyel/khtyela ysem*
This isn't clean	**Není to čisté**	*nenyee to chistai*
This smells bad	**Zapáchá to**	*zapaakhaa to*
We've been waiting too long	**Čekáme moc dlouho**	*chekaame mots dloh-ho*
There is a mistake on the bill	**V účtu je chyba**	*f oochtu ye khiba*

In shops

I bought this here (yesterday)	**Koupil jsem to tady (včera)**	*kohpil ysem to tadi (fchera)*
Can I change this?	**Můžete mi to vyměnit?**	*moozhete mi to vimnyenyit*
I want to return this	**Chtěl** (male)/**Chtěla** (female) **bych to vrátit**	*khtyel/khtyela bikh to vraatyit*
Can I have a refund?	**Můžu dostat zpátky peníze?**	*moozhu dostat spaatki penyeeze*
It has a flaw in it	**Má to vadu**	*maa to vadu*
There is a stain	**Má to skvrnu**	*maa to skvrnu*
This is off/rotten	**Je to prošlé/zkažené**	*ye to proshlai/skazhenai*
This is past its sell-by date	**Má to prošlou záruční lhůtu**	*maa to proshloh zaaruchnyee lhootu*

Forgetting things and theft

I've forgotten ...	Zapomněl (male)/ Zapomněla (female) jsem ...	zapomnyel/ zapomnyela ysem
... the tickets/key	... lístky/klíč	leestki/kleech
I left my ... here yesterday/ this morning	Zapomněl (male)/ Zapomněla (female) jsem tu včera/dnes ráno ...	zapomnyel/ zapomnyela ysem tu fchera/dnes raano
... glasses/documents/keys/ watch	... brýle/dokumenty/ klíče/hodinky	breele/dokumenti/ kleeche/hodyinki
I've lost ...	Ztratil (male)/Ztratila (female) jsem ...	stratyil/stratyila ysem
... my wallet/driving licence/ passport	... peněženku/řidičský průkaz/pas	penyezhenku/ rzhidyichskee prookas/ pas
Where is the lost property office?	Kde jsou ztráty a nálezy?	gde ysoh straati a naalezi
Where is the police station?	Kde je policejní stanice?	gde ye politseynyee stanyitse
Someone has stolen my ... ... bag/money/passport	Někdo mi ukradl ... tašku/peníze/pas	nyegdo mi ukradl tashku/penyeeze/pas

If someone is bothering you

Please, leave me alone	Nechte mě na pokoji prosím	nekhte mnye na pokoyi proseem
Go away or I'll call the police	Odejděte, nebo zavolám policii	odeydyete nebo zavolaam politsiyi
There is someone bothering me	Někdo mě obtěžuje	nyegdo mnye optyezhuye
There is someone following me	Někdo mě sleduje	nyegdo mnye sleduye

You may hear

Helpful and unhelpful remarks

Počkejte chvíli prosím	*poch*keyte *khvee*li proseem	Wait a moment, please
Okamžik	*okam*zhik	Just a minute
Prosím	*pro*seem	Here you are
Bohužel, ...	*bo*huzhel	Unfortunately, ...
... nedá se nic dělat	nedaa se *nyits dye*lat	... nothing can be done
... je pozdě	ye *pozd*ye	... it's too late
Nejde to	*ney*de to	It's not possible
Nevím	ne*veem*	I don't know
To není moje/naše vina.	to nenyee *mo*ye/*na*she vina	I am/We are not responsible

Questions you may be asked

Kdy/Kde jste to ztratil (male)/**ztratila** (female)?	*gdi*/*gde* yste to *stra*tyil/ *stra*tyila	When/Where did you lose it?
Kdy/Kde/Jak se to stalo?	*gdi*/*gde*/*yak* se to *sta*lo	When/Where/How did it happen?
Jak vypadá ...	*yak* vi*pa*daa	What does ... look like?
... to auto	to auto	... the car ...
... ten kufr	ten *kufr*	... the suitcase ...
... ta taška	ta *tash*ka	... the bag ...
Vyplňte prosím tento formulář	*vipl*nyte proseem *ten*to *for*mulaarzh	Please fill in this form
Vaše doklady prosím	*va*she *do*kladi proseem	Your documents, please

(See also PROBLEMS AND COMPLAINTS, page 113)

You may want to say

Phoning the emergency services

I need ...	**Potřebuji ...**	*potrzhebuyi*
... the police	**... policii**	*politsiyi*
... the fire brigade	**... hasiče**	*hasiche*
... an ambulance	**... záchranku**	*zaachranku*
There's a fire	**Hoří**	*horzhee*
There's been an accident	**Stala se nehoda**	*stala se nehoda*
There's been a car accident	**Stala se autonehoda**	*stala se autonehoda*
It's my husband/son	**Jde o manžela/syna**	*yde o manzhela/sina*
It's my wife/daughter	**Jde o manželku/dceru**	*yde o manzhelku/tseru*
He/She is seriously injured	**Má vážné zranění**	*maa vaazhnai zranyenyee*
He/She is bleeding	**Krvácí**	*krvaatsee*
He/She is unconscious	**Je v bezvědomí**	*ye v bezvyedomee*
Please come immediately	**Přijeďte ihned**	*przhiyedyte ihnet*
Where is the police station?	**Kde je policejní stanice?**	*gde ye politseynyee stanyitse*
Where is the hospital?	**Kde je nemocnice?**	*gde ye nemotsnyitse*

Emergency exclamations

Help!	**Pomoc!**	*pomots*
Police!	**Policii!**	*politsiyi*

Get out of the way!	**Z cesty!**	*s tsesti*
Call the fire brigade!	**Zavolejte hasiče!**	*zavoleyte hasiche*
Call an ambulance!	**Zavolejte záchranku!**	*zavoleyte zaakhranku*
Stop thief!	**Zastavte zloděje!**	*zastafte zlodyeye*
Look out!	**Pozor!**	*pozor*
Fire!	**Hoří!**	*horzhee*
Get a doctor	**(Zavolejte) doktora!**	*zavoleyte doktora*
Get help quickly	**Zavolejte rychle pomoc**	*zavoleyte rikhle pomots*
It's an emergency	**Je to naléhavý případ**	*ye to nalaihavee przheepat*

Emergency telephone numbers

158	Police	0149	International operator
155	Ambulance		
150	Fire		
154	Car breakdown and tow-away service		

I need the number for ...	**Potřebuji číslo ...**	*potrzhebuyi cheeslo*
Police	**Policie**	*politsiye*
Fire brigade	**Hasičů**	*hasichoo*
Ambulance	**Ambulance**	*ambulantse*

You may hear

When you phone the emergency services

Co se stalo?	*tso se stalo*	What happened?
Jméno a adresu prosím	*ymaino a adresu proseem*	Your name and address please
Posíláme někoho	*poseelaame nyekoho*	We're sending someone
Hasičský vůz/Sanitka je na cestě	*hasichskee voos/ sanitka ye na tsestye*	A fire engine/An ambulance is on its way

Numbers

Cardinals

▌ Numerals **jeden** (one) and **dva** (two) are followed by a masculine noun: **jeden muž** (one man), **dva muži** (two men), while **jedna** and **dvě** are followed by a feminine noun: **jedna žena** (one woman), **dvě ženy** (two women). For more information about gender, see BASIC GRAMMAR, page 12). The two neuter forms are **jedno** and **dvě**.

▌ The word following the numerals has two different forms: one following **dva, tři,** and **čtyři** (two, three, and four) and the other following **pět** (five) upwards.

0	**nula**	*nula*	18	**osmnáct**	*osmnaatst*
1	**jeden**	*yeden*	19	**devatenáct**	*devatenaatst*
2	**dva**	*dva*	20	**dvacet**	*dvatset*
3	**tři**	*trzhi*	21 etc.	**dvacet jedna**	*dvatset yedna*
4	**čtyři**	*chtirzhi*	30	**třicet**	*trzhitset*
5	**pět**	*pyet*	31 etc.	**třicet jedna**	*trzhitset yedna*
6	**šest**	*shest*	40	**čtyřicet**	*chtirzhitset*
7	**sedm**	*sedm*	50	**padesát**	*padesaat*
8	**osm**	*osm*	60	**šedesát**	*shedesaat*
9	**devět**	*devyet*	70	**sedmdesát**	*sedmdesaat*
10	**deset**	*deset*	80	**osmdesát**	*osmdesaat*
11	**jedenáct**	*jedenaatst*	90	**devadesát**	*devadesaat*
12	**dvanáct**	*dvanaatst*	100	**sto**	*sto*
13	**třináct**	*trzhinaatst*	101 etc.	**sto jedna**	*sto yedna*
14	**čtrnáct**	*chtrnaatst*	200	**dvě stě**	*dvye stye*
15	**patnáct**	*patnaatst*	300	**tři sta**	*trzhi sta*
16	**šestnáct**	*shestnaatst*	400	**čtyři sta**	*chtirzhi sta*
17	**sedmnáct**	*sedmnaatst*	500	**pět set**	*pyet set*

600	**šest set**	*shest set*
700	**sedm set**	*sedm set*
800	**osm set**	*osm set*
900	**devět set**	*devyet set*
1,000	**tisíc**	*tyiseets*
2,000	**dva tisíce**	*dva tyiseetse*
5,000	**pět tisíc**	*pyet tyiseets*
1,000,000	**milión**	*miliawn*
2,000,000	**dva milióny**	*dva miliawni*
5,000,000	**pět miliónů**	*pyet miliawnoo*

Ordinals

▮ These words have different endings for masculine, feminine and neuter nouns which follow them (see BASIC GRAMMAR, page 12). In writing, ordinals are distinguished from cardinals by a full stop, e.g. 21 is twenty-one, but 21. means 21st.

▮ The list below includes the form to be used with masculine nouns (**druhý den** – the second day). To combine these words with feminine and neuter nouns, replace the ending **-ý** with **-á** and **-é** respectively (**sedmá strana** – the seventh page, **čtvrté kolo** – the fourth wheel). The next column lists words to be used in expressions such as: **prvního dubna** (the 1st of April) (see also DAYS, MONTHS, DATES, page 126). Use the words in the last column in telling the time after **půl** (half past), **po** (after), **kolem** (at about) etc. (See also TIME, page 124).

			Words to be used in dates	Words to be used in telling the time
1st	**první**	*prvnyee*	**prvního**	**jedné**
2nd	**druhý**	*druhee*	**druhého**	**druhé**
3rd	**třetí**	*trzhetyee*	**třetího**	**třetí**
4th	**čtvrtý**	*chtvrtee*	**čtvrtého**	**čtvrté**

			Words to be used in dates	Words to be used in telling the time
5th	pátý	*paatee*	pátého	páté
6th	šestý	*shestee*	šestého	šesté
7th	sedmý	*sedmee*	sedmého	sedmé
8th	osmý	*osmee*	osmého	osmé
9th	devátý	*devaatee*	devátého	deváté
10th	desátý	*desaatee*	desátého	desáté
11th	jedenáctý	*yedenaatstee*	jedenáctého	jedenácté
12th	dvanáctý	*dvanaatstee*	dvanáctého	dvanácté
13th	třináctý	*trzhinaatstee*	třináctého	
14th	čtrnáctý	*chtrnaatstee*	čtrnáctého	
15th	patnáctý	*patnaatstee*	patnáctého	
16th	šestnáctý	*shestnaatstee*	šestnáctého	
17th	sedmnáctý	*sedmnaatstee*	sedmnáctého	
18th	osmnáctý	*osmnaatstee*	osmnáctého	
19th	devatenáctý	*devatenaatstee*	devatenáctého	
20th	dvacátý	*dvatsaatee*	dvacátého	
21st etc.	dvacátý první	*dvatsaatee prvnyee*	dvacátého prvního etc.	
30th	třicáty	*trzhitsaatee*	třicátého etc.	
40th	čtyřicátý	*chtirzhitsaatee*		
50th	padesátý	*padesaatee*		
60th	šedesátý	*shedesaatee*		
70th	sedmdesátý	*sedmdesaatee*		
80th	osmdesátý	*osmdesaatee*		
90th	devadesátý	*devadesaatee*		
100th	stý	*stee*		
200th	dvoustý	*dvohstee*		
300th etc.	třístý	*trheestee*		
1,000th	tisící	*tyiseetsee*		

123

(See also NUMBERS, page 121)

❚ Time is normally expressed with the 12-hour clock. Sometimes the words **ráno** (early in the morning until about 9 a.m.), **dopoledne** (in the morning), **odpoledne** (in the afternoon) or **večer** (in the evening) are added. The 24-hour clock is used for public transport, in the media and more formally. **Hodina** means both 'o'clock' and 'hour'.

❚ Both cardinal (one, two, three, etc.) and ordinal (first, second, third, etc.) numerals are used in giving the time. The ordinals following **půl** (half past) take the ending -**é** (e.g. **sedm-ý** becomes **sedm-é**: half past six = **půl sedmé**).

❚ To say that it's half past something in Czech you have to say that it's half way round to the next hour, e.g. half past six is **půl sedmé**, because it's half way round to seven.

❚ Telling the time in Czech is different from English and rather complicated. You may avoid grammatical pitfalls if you tell the time as it appears on a digital clock. It is perfectly all right if you say **v šest dvacet pět** (at six twenty-five) and add **ráno** (in the morning) or **večer** (in the evening) if necessary.

You may want to say

What's the time?	**Kolik je hodin?**	kolik ye hodyin
It's ...	**Je...**	ye
... one o'clock	... **jedna hodina**	**yed**na **ho**dyina
It's ...	**Jsou ...**	ysoh
... two/three/four o'clock	... **dvě/tři/čtyři hodiny**	**dvye/trzhi/chti**rzhi **ho**dyini
It's ...	**Je ...**	ye
... five/six/12 o'clock	... **pět/šest/dvanáct hodin**	**pyet/shest/dva**naatst **ho**dyin

It's ...	Je ...	ye
... a quarter past ...	... čtvrt na ... (+ the *next* whole hour in cardinals)	chtvrt na
... a quarter past five	... čtvrt na šest	chtvrt na shest
... half past ...	... půl ... (+ the *next* whole hour in ordinals)	pool
... half past five	... půl šesté	pool shestai
... five/10 (minutes) past seven	... sedm (hodin) pět/ deset (minut)	sedm hodyin pyet/deset minut
... a quarter to ...	... třičtvrtě na ... (cardinals)	trzhichtvrtye na
... a quarter to 10	... třičtvrtě na deset	trzhichtvrtye na deset
... 9.45	... devět čtyřicet pět	devyet chtirzhitset pyet
... ten/20 to ...	za deset/dvacet (minut) ... (cardinals)	za deset/dvatset minut
... 10 to four	za deset čtyři	za deset chtirzhi
In the morning (a.m.)	dopoledne	dopoledne
In the early morning	ráno	raano
This morning	dnes ráno/dopoledne	dnes raano/dopoledne
In the afternoon	odpoledne	otpoledne
This afternoon	dnes odpoledne	dnes otpoledne
In the evening	večer	vecher
Tonight (early)	dnes večer	dnes vecher
Tonight (late)	dnes v noci	dnes v notsi
A quarter of an hour	čtvrthodina	chtvrthodyina
Three quarters of an hour	tři čtvrtě hodiny	trzhi chtvrtye hodyini
Half an hour	půlhodina	poolhodyina
(At) what time?	V kolik hodin?	f kolik hodyin
At ...	v..., ve ...	v/f, ve
At half past one	V půl druhé	f pool druhai
At a quarter to seven	Ve třičtvrtě na sedm	ve trzhichtvrtye na sedm
At about ...	kolem ... (ordinals)	kolem ...

125

(See also NUMBERS, page 121)

▌ Days and months are written with small letters. The numeral in dates is always followed by a full stop, e.g. **20. ledna 1996**, to indicate that it is an ordinal.

▌ To say the date, use the formula: ordinal numeral (**dvacát-ý**) + ending: **-ého** + month. The correct form of each month as it should appear in this phrase is listed in brackets below.

Days

Monday/On Monday	**pondělí/v pondělí**	*pondyelee/f pondyelee*
Tuesday/On Tuesday	**úterý/v úterý**	*ooteree/f ooteree*
Wednesday/On Wednesday	**středa/ve středu**	*strzheda/ve strzhedu*
Thursday/On Thursday	**čtvrtek/ve čtvrtek**	*chtvrtek/ve chtvrtek*
Friday/On Friday	**pátek/v pátek**	*paatek/f paatek*
Saturday/On Saturday	**sobota/v sobotu**	*sobota/f sobotu*
Sunday/On Sunday	**neděle/v neděli**	*nedyele/v nedyeli*

Months

January/In January	**leden/v lednu (ledna)**	*leden/v lednu (ledna)*
February/In February	**únor/v únoru (února)**	*oonor/v oonoru (oonora)*
March/In March	**březen/v březnu (března)**	*brzhezen/v brzheznu (brzhezna)*
April/In April	**duben/v dubnu (dubna)**	*duben/v dubnu (dubna)*
May/In May	**květen/v květnu (května)**	*kvyeten/f kvyetnu (kvyetna)*
June/In June	**červen/v červnu (června)**	*cherven/f chervnu (chervna)*

July/In July	**červenec/v červenci** (července)	*chervenets/f cherventsi* (*cherventse*)
August/In August	**srpen/v srpnu (srpna)**	*srpen/f srpnu (srpna)*
September/In September	**září/v září (září)**	*zaarzhee/v zaarzhee* (*zaarzhee*)
October/In October	**říjen/v říjnu (října)**	*rzheeyen/v rzheeynu* (*rzheeyna*)
November/In November	**listopad/v listopadu** (listopadu)	*listopat/v listopadu* (*listopadu*)
December/In December	**prosinec/v prosinci** (prosince)	*prosinets/f prosintsi* (*prosintse*)

Seasons

Spring/In spring	**jaro/na jaře**	*yaro/na yarzhe*
Summer/In summer	**léto/v létě**	*laito/v laitye*
Autumn/In autumn	**podzim/na podzim**	*podzim/na podzim*
Winter/In winter	**zima/v zimě**	*zima/v zimnye*

General phrases

day	**den**	*den*
two/three/four days	**dva/tři/čtyři dny**	*dva/trzhi/chtirzhi dni*
five/six days	**pět/šest dní**	*pyet/shest dnyee*
week	**týden**	*teeden*
two/three/four weeks	**dva/tři/čtyři týdny**	*dva/trzhi/chtirzhi teedni*
five/six weeks	**pět/šest týdnů**	*pyet/shest teednoo*
fortnight	**čtrnáct dní**	*chtrnaatst dnyee*
month	**měsíc**	*mnyeseets*
two/three/four months	**dva/tři/čtyři měsíce**	*dva/trzhi/chtirzhi mnyeseetse*

127

English	Czech	Pronunciation
five/six months	pět/šest měsíců	pyet/shest mnyeseetsoo
year	rok	rok
two/three/four years	dva/tři/čtyři roky	dva/trzhi/chtirzhi roki
five/six years	pět/šest roků	pyet/shest rokoo
(in) the (early) morning	ráno	raano
(in) the morning (a.m.)	dopoledne	dopoledne
(in) the afternoon	odpoledne	otpoledne
(in) the evening	večer	vecher
at night	v noci	v notsi
tonight	dnes večer	dnes vecher
tomorrow morning (early)	zítra ráno	zeetra raano
tomorrow morning (a.m.)	zítra dopoledne	zeetra dopoledne
yesterday afternoon/ evening	včera odpoledne/ večer	fchera otpoledne/ vecher
last night	včera v noci	fchera v notsi
every Tuesday/Tuesdays	každé úterý	kazhdai ooteree
last ...	minulý	minulee
last Monday/Tuesday	minulé pondělí/úterý	minulai pondyelee/ ooteree
last Wednesday/Saturday/ Sunday	minulou středu/sobotu/ neděli	minuloh strzhedu/sobotu/ nedyeli
last Thursday/Friday	minulý čtvrtek/pátek	minulee chtvrtek/paatek
last week	minulý týden	minulee teeden
last month	minulý měsíc	minulee mnyeseets
last year	minulý rok/loni	minulee rok/lonyi
next ...	příští ...	przheeshtyee
next Tuesday/week month/year	příští úterý/týden měsíc/rok	przheeshtyee ooteree/ teeden mnyeseets/ rok
What day is it today?	Co je dnes za den?	tso ye dnes za den
What is the date today?	Kolikátého je dnes?	kolikaataiho ye dnes

Countries and nationalities

▌ It is usual in Czech to refer to someone's nationality by saying **On je Angličan** (he is an Englishman), rather than 'he is English'. There are two words ro refer to a person from a country, depending on whether it's a male or a female: **Angličan** (Englishman), **Angličanka** (Englishwoman). The adjective **anglický** (English) changes its ending according to gender: **anglický jazyk** (English language), **anglická snídaně** (English breakfast), **anglické město** (English town). The same word with **-y** at the end is used to say you speak a language (**anglický – anglicky**), however in this case it remains unchanged: **Mluvím česky/anglicky/německy/francouzsky** etc. (I speak Czech/English/German/French etc.). Only words referring to a member of a nation are written with a capital letter.

Country (English name)	Country (Czech name)	Nationality (masculine, feminine, and masculine adj.)
America	Amerika	Američan, Američanka, americký
Australia	Austrálie	Australan, Australanka, australský
Belgium	Belgie	Belgičan, Belgičanka, belgický
Bulgaria	Bulharsko	Bulhar, Bulharka, bulharský
Bosnia	Bosna	Bosňan, Bosňanka, bosenský
Canada	Kanada	Kanaďan, Kanaďanka, kanadský
Croatia	Chorvatsko	Chorvat, Chorvatka, chorvatský
Czech Republic	Česká republika	Čech, Češka, český
Denmark	Dánsko	Dán, Dánka, dánský
England	Anglie	Angličan, Angličanka, anglický
Europe	Evropa	Evropan, Evropanka, evropský
Finland	Finsko	Fin, Finka, finský
France	Francie	Francouz, Francouzka, francouzský
Germany	Německo	Němec, Němka, německý
Great Britain	Velká Británie	Brit, Britka, britský

Greece	Řecko	Řek, Řekyně, řecký
Holland	Holandsko	Holanďan, Holanďanka, holandský
Hungary	Maďarsko	Maďar, Maďarka, maďarský
Ireland	Irsko	Ir, Irka, irský
Italy	Itálie	Ital, Italka, italský
Luxembourg	Lucembursko	Lucemburčan, Lucemburčanka, lucemburský
Macedonia	Makedonie	Makedonec, Makedonka, makedonský
Netherlands	Nizozemsko	Nizozemec, Nizozemka, nizozemský
New Zealand	Nový Zéland	Novozélanďan, Novozélanďanka, novozélandský
North America	Severní Amerika	Severoameričan, Severoameričanka, severoamerický
Northern Ireland	Severní Irsko	Ir, Irka ze (from) Severního Irska, severoirský
Norway	Norsko	Nor, Norka, norský
Poland	Polsko	Polák, Polka, polsky
Portugal	Portugalsko	Portugalec, Portugalka, portugalský
Romania	Rumunsko	Rumun, Rumunka, rumunský
Russia	Rusko	Rus, Ruska, ruský
Scotland	Skotsko	Skot, Skotka, skotský
Slovak Republic/ Slovakia	Slovenská republika Slovensko	Slovák, Slovenka, slovenský
Slovenia	Slovinsko	Slovinec, Slovinka, slovinský
Spain	Španělsko	Španěl, Španělka, španělský
Sweden	Švédsko	Švéd, Švédka, švédský
Switzerland	Švýcarsko	Švýcar, Švýcarka, švýcarský
Turkey	Turecko	Turek, Turkyně, turecký
Ukraine	Ukrajina	Ukrajinec, Ukrajinka, ukrajinský
United Kingdom	Spojené království (Velké Británie a Severniko Irska)	
United States	Spojené státy	Američan, Američanka, americký
Wales	Wales	Velšan, Velšanka, velšský

General signs and notices

Cyklistická stezka	Cycle path
Ceník	Price list
Čekárna	Waiting room
Čekejte na vyzvání	Wait until you are called
Čerstvě natřeno	Wet paint
Dámy	Ladies (toilets)
Datum výroby	Date of manufacture (see SHOPPING, page 89)
Datum spotřeby	Use-by date
Dovolená	Closed for staff leave
DPH	VAT
Horká	Hot
Informace	Information
Klepejte	Please knock
Kouření zakázáno	No smoking
Kuřáci	Smokers
Mimo provoz	Closed/Out of order
Místa k stání	Standing places
Muži	Men (toilets)
Na prodej	For sale
Na vlastní nebezpečí	At your own risk
Návod k použití	Instructions for use
Návštěvní hodiny	Visiting hours
Nebezpečí požáru	Fire hazard
Nebezpečí úrazu	Danger of accident
Nedotýkejte se	Do not touch
Nehodící se škrtněte	Delete where inapplicable
Nekuřáci	Non-smokers

Nemluvte za jízdy s řidičem	Do not speak to the driver when the vehicle is in motion
Neopírejte se o dveře	Do not lean against the door
Nepovolaným vstup zakázán	Admission for authorised persons only
Nevstupovat	No entry
Nouzový východ	Emergency exit
Obsazeno	Engaged
Obsazeno (in a hotel)	No vacancies
Otevřeno	Open
Otvírací doba	Opening hours
Páni	Gents (toilets)
Záchody	Toilets
Zadáno	Reserved
Zákaz koupání	No bathing
Zavřeno	Closed
Zvoňte	Ring the bell
Ženy	Women (toilets)

Conversion tables

All measurements are approximate equivalents.

Linear measurements

centimetres **centimetry (cm)**
metres **metry (m)**
kilometres **kilometry (km)**

10 cm	= 4 inches	1 inch = 2.54 cm
50 cm	= 19.6 inches	1 foot = 30 cm
1 metre	= 39.37 inches	1 yard = 0.91 cm
(just over 1 yard)		
110 metres	= 100 yards	
1 km	= 0.62 miles	1 mile = 1.61 km

To convert:

km to miles: divide by 8 and multiply by 5

miles to km: divide by 5 and multiply by 8

Miles/Kilometres

miles		kilometres	miles		kilometres
0.6	1	1.6	19	30	48
1.2	2	3.2	25	40	64
1.9	3	4.8	31	50	80
2.5	4	6.4	62	100	161
3	5	8	68	110	177
6	10	16	75	120	193
12	20	32	81	130	209

Liquid measurements

litre **litr (l)**

1 litre	= 1.8 pints		1 pint	= 0.57 litres
5 litres	= 1.1 gallons		1 gallon	= 4.55 litres

One litre of water is one and three-quarter pints

Note: 1 litre equals 10 decilitres (dl). Decilitres, or **deci** for short, are sometimes used, e.g. when ordering wine in a restaurant. One glass of wine is approximately 2 decilitres (or 7 fl. oz), or **dvě deci vína**.

Gallons/Litres

gallons		litres	gallons		litres
0.2	1	4.5	0.9	4	18
0.4	2	9	1.1	5	23
0.7	3	13.6	2.2	10	45.5

Weights

gram	**gram (g)**	
100 grams	**sto gramů**	
200 grams	**dvě stě gramů**	
kilo	**kilogram (kg)**	

100 g	= 3.5 oz	1 oz	= 28 g
200 g	= 7 oz	1/4 lb	= 113 g
1/2 kg	= 1.1 lb	1/2 lb	= 227 g
1 kg	= 2.2 lb	1 lb	= 453 g

Note: 1 kilogram equals 100 dekagrams (dkg). Dekagrams, or **deka** for short, are used when buying food which has to be weighed, such as cheese, salami, and various delicatessen items. To buy approximately a quarter pound of ham you will ask for **deset deka šunky**,

Pounds/Kilos

pounds		kilos	pounds		kilos
2.2	1	0.45 (450)	8.8	4	1.8 (1800)
4.4	2	0.9 (900)	11	5	2.3 (2300)
6.6	3	1.4 (1400)	22	10	4.5 (4500)

Clothing and shoe sizes

Women's dresses and suits

UK	10	12	14	16	18	20
Continental	36	38	40	42	44	46

Men's suits and coats

UK	36	38	40	42	44	46
Continental	46	48	50	52	54	56

Men's shirts

UK	14	14½	15	15½	16	16½	17	17½	18
Continental	36	37	38	39	40	41	42	43	44

Shoes

UK	2	3	4	5	6	7	8	9	10	11
Continental	35	36	37	38	39	41	42	43	44	45

Waist and chest measurements

in	28	30	32	34	36	38	40	42	44	46	48	50
cm	71	76	81	87	91	97	102	107	112	117	122	127

Tyre pressure

lb/sq in	15	18	20	22	24	26	28	30	33	35
kg/sq cm	1.1	1.3	1.4	1.5	1.7	1.8	2.0	2.1	2.3	2.5

Nový rok	New Year's Day	1 January
Velikonoční pondělí	Easter Monday	
Svátek práce	Labour Day	1 May
Den osvobození od fašismu	Day of liberation from fascism	8 May
Den Cyrila a Metoděje	Cyril and Methodius (Slavonic missionaries) Day	5 July
Den Mistra Jana Husa	Jan Hus (religious reformer) Day	6 July
Den vzniku samostatného Československa	Founding of independent Czechoslovakia	28 October
Štědrý den	Christmas Eve	24 December
1.svátek vánoční	First Christmas holiday	25 December
2.svátek vánoční	Second Christmas holiday	26 December

Useful addresses

In the UK

Czech Embassy
26 Kensington Palace Gardens
London W8 4QY
tel. 0171–243 1115

Czech Consulate
26 Kensington Palace Gardens
London W8 4QY
tel. 0171–243 7919

**Czech Cultural and
Information Centre**
30 Kensington Palace Gardens
London W8 4QY
tel. 0171–243 7981/2

Czech Tourist Centre
178 Finchley Road
London NW3 6BP
tel. 0171–794 3263/4

Čedok Travel Ltd.
53/54 Haymarket
London SW1Y 4RP
tel. 0171–839 4414

Czechoslovak Airlines (CSA)
72 Margaret Street
London W1N 8HA
tel. 0171–255 1898

In the Czech Republic

British Embassy
Thunovská 14
Praha 1
tel. 2451 0439

American Embassy
Tržiště 15
Praha 1
tel. 2451 0847

Canadian Embassy
Mickiewiczova 6
Praha 6
tel. 2431 1108

British Cultural Centre
Britské kulturní středisko
Národní 10
Praha 1
tel. 2491 2179

American Cultural Centre
Americké kulturní středisko
Hybernská 7a
Praha 1
tel. 2423 1085

Prague Information Service PIS
Pražská informační služba
Na příkopě 20
Praha 1
tel. 54 44 44

Foreigners' and Border Police
Cizinecká a pohraniční policie
Olšanská 2
Praha 3
tel. 3354 1111

Foreigners' Medical Centre
Nemocnice Na Homolce
Roentgenova ul.
Praha 5
tel. 5292 2146

Čedok Travel Ltd.
Na příkopě 18
Praha 1
tel. 2419 7111

General Customs Head Office
Ústřední celní správa
Praha 1
tel. 2406 1111
Václavské náměstí 57

In the US

Czech Embassy
3900 Spring of Freedom St, NW
Washington DC 20008
tel. 202–363 6315

Čedok Travel Ltd
10 E 40th St
New York NY 10157
tel. 212–689 9720

In Canada

Czech Embassy
541 Sussex Drive
Ottawa, Ontario K1N 6Z6
tel. 613–562 3875

In Australia

Czech Embassy
(for Australia and New Zealand)
38 Culgoa Circuit, O'Malley
Canberra ACT 2606
tel. 62901386

In Ireland

Czech Embassy
57 Northumberland Road
Ballabridge
Dublin 4
tel. 2–6681135

Useful and emergency telephone numbers

150 Fire   **123, 154** Car breakdown and towaway service

155 Ambulance   **42 41 41** Traffic police – road accidents (24-hour service)

158 Police

- Directory enquiries:

120 for numbers in Prague

121 for numbers in the Czech Republic

0139 Information on international telephone rates and services

0149 for international numbers

- To make an international call dial: 00 + country code + area code + the number.

Some country codes when calling from the Czech Republic:

UK	00 44	UK operator (for reverse-charge calls) 00 42 00 44 01
Ireland	00 353	
USA and Canada	00 1	
Australia	00 61	
New Zealand	00 64	

The country code for the Czech Republic (when calling from abroad): 00 42

Prague area code: 02 (or 2 when calling from abroad)

- Information:

(Prague numbers)

General information PIS	54 44 44 – 7
Information on public transport	29 46 82, 2422 5135
Information for motorists (**Automotoklub**)	123, 0123
Information on coach and bus transport, Prague – Florenc main coach station	2421 1060 – 67
Air travel information service, Prague-Ruzyně international airport	36 78 14

English-Czech Dictionary

▌The following word lists can be referred to in this book:

food – in MENU READER	page 80
car parts and road signs – in ROAD TRAVEL	page 36
parts of the body – in HEALTH	page 106
nationalities – in COUNTRIES AND NATIONALITIES	page 129

▌Czech verbs appear in two forms: the imperfective describing continuous, uncompleted or repetitive action, and the perfective for a single or completed action (e.g. *Dělal* **chyby**/imperfective – He made mistakes; *Udělal* **chybu**/perfective – He made a mistake). In this Dictionary, the form which you will be most likely to use is given. In some instances the alternative form is listed separately (to phone – **telefonovat**, to make a call – **zatelefonovat si**).

▌All verbs listed in the Dictionary begin with 'to'. For some hints on how to form sentences with these verbs, see BASIC GRAMMAR, page 12.

▌Where two Czech equivalents are given (especially for occupations, or other words relating to human beings) the first is the male form, and the second the female form.

▌All Czech nouns, including those that relate to inanimate objects and abstract notions, have one of the three genders: masculine, feminine or neuter. In this Dictionary, the gender is indicated by abbreviations *m*, *f*, and *n* following the nouns, except where the gender is obvious (e.g. son, king).

▌Adjectives (words like hot, light, small) ending in -ý have different endings for masculine (-ý), feminine (-á), and neuter (-é) genders. Listed below are only masculine forms. These changes do not occur with adjectives ending in -í (see also BASIC GRAMMAR, page 12).

▌To combine an adjective and a noun (light + colour), change the adjective ending -ý to match the gender of the noun (e.g. light = **světlý**, colour = **barva** *f*, light colour = **světlá barva**).

■ If a Czech noun has a plural form where the English equivalent is in singular, and vice versa, it is noted by abbreviations *sg* and *pl*. For example the words **dveře** (door) and **šaty** (dress) are followed by **jsou** (are) even if they refer to one object only. On the other hand, 'peas' translates as **hrášek**, and is followed by **je** (is).

■ Some pronouns and their forms (I, me, my, he, him, his, etc.) are listed below. Others can be found in BASIC GRAMMAR, page 12.

A

about (relating to)	**o**
about (approximately)	**asi**
above	**nad**
abroad (to be abroad)	**v zahraničí** n
abroad (to go abroad)	**do zahraničí**
abscess	**absces** m
to accept (take)	**přijmout**
accident	**nehoda** f
accommodation	**ubytování** n
according to	**podle**
account (bank)	**účet** m
ache/pain	**bolest** f
across (to go across)	**přes**
across (on the other side)	**na druhé straně** f
activity	**činnost** f
adaptor (voltage)	**adaptér** m
adaptor (multiple plug)	**rozdvojka** f
address	**adresa** f

adhesive tape	**lepicí páska** f
admission (charge)	**vstupné** n
adult	**dospělý** m
advance: in advance	**předem**
advanced (level)	**pokročilý**
advertisement	**inzerát** m
aerial	**anténa** f
afford: I can't afford it	**nemám na to**
afraid: to be afraid	**bát se**
after	**po**
afternoon	**odpoledne** n
after-shave	**voda** f **po holení**
again	**znovu**
against	**proti**
age	**věk** m
agency: travel agency	**cestovní kancelář** f
ago	**před**
many years ago	**před mnoha lety**
to agree (price)	**dohodnout**
air	**vzduch** m
air-conditioning	**klimatizace** f

airline	**aerolinky** *pl*	animal	**zvíře** *n*
airport	**letiště** *n*	anniversary	**výročí** *n*
alarm clock	**budík** *m*	anorak	**větrovka** *f*
alive	**živý**	another (one)	**ještě jeden**
all (people)	**všichni**	answer	**odpověď** *f*
all (everything)	**všechno**	to answer	**odpovědět**
to allow	**dovolit**	antibiotic	**antibiotikum** *n*
allowed	**dovoleno**	anti-freeze	**nemrznoucí směs**
all right	**v pořádku**		
almond	**mandle** *f*	antique	**starožitnost** *f*
alone	**sám** *m*, **sama** *f*, **samo** *n*	antique shop	**starožitonosti** *pl*
		any (some)	**nějaký**
along	**podél**	anyone (someone)	**někdo**
already	**už**	anything (something)	**něco**
also	**také**		
always	**vždycky**	anyway	**v každém případě**
am (I am)	**(já) jsem**		
ambulance	**sanitka** *f* **záchranka** *f*	anywhere (somewhere)	**někde**
among	**mezi**	apart (from)	**kromě**
amount (of money)	**částka** *f*	apartment (hotel)	**apartmá** *n*
		apartment (flat)	**byt** *m*
amount (quantity)	**množství** *n*	appendicitis	**zánět** *m* **slepého střeva**
amusement park	**zábavní park** *m*		
analgesic	**prostředek** *m* **na utišení bolesti**	apple	**jablko** *n*
		appointment	**schůzka** *f*
anaesthetic (general)	**narkóza** *f*	to make a doctor's appointment	**objednat se u lékaře**
anaesthetic (local)	**lokální umrtvení** *n*		
		approximately	**přibližně**
and	**a**	apricot	**meruňka** *f*
angling	**rybaření** *n*	are (they are)	**(oni) jsou**
		area	**oblast** *f*

argument (row)	**hádka** f
army	**armáda** f
around	**kolem**
to arrange	**zařídit**
to arrest	**zatknout**
arrival (by land)	**příjezd** m
arrival (by air)	**přílet** m
to arrive (on foot)	**přijít**
to arrive (by land)	**přijet** m
to arrive (by air)	**přiletět**
art/fine arts	**umění** n/**krásná umění**
art gallery	**umělecká galerie** f
artificial	**umělý**
as (like)	**jako**
as far as (a place)	**až do**
ashtray	**popelník** m
to ask (a question)	**zeptat se**
to ask (for something)	**požádat (o)**
as well	**také**
at (be at)	**v, na**
at (arrive at)	**do, na**
at once	**hned**
to attack	**útočit**
aunt	**teta**
autumn	**podzim** m
to avoid	**vyhnout se**
away (be/go)	**pryč**

(... km) away from here	**(km) odsud**
awful	**strašný**

B

baby	**miminko** n
baby cereal	**dětská kaše** f
baby food	**kojenecká strava** f
baby's bottle	**kojenecká láhev** f
babysitter	**někdo na hlídání**
back: to go back	**vrátit se**
at the back	**vzadu**
bacon	**slanina** f
bad	**špatný**
bag	**taška** f
baker's	**pekařství** n
balcony	**balkón** m
ball	**míč** m
ballpoint pen	**propisovačka** f
band (music)	**kapela** f
bandage	**obvaz** m
barber's	**holič** m/**holičství** n
basement	**suterén** m
basket	**košík** m
basketball	**košíková** f
bath (tub)	**vana** f
to have a bath	**vykoupat se**
bathroom	**koupelna** f
battery	**baterie** f
to be	**být**

ach	**pláž** f	bill	**účet** m
bean	**fazole** f	bin	**odpadkový koš** m
beard	**vousy** pl	binoculars	**dalekohled** m sg
beautiful	**krásný**	bird	**pták** m
because	**protože**	birthday	**narozeniny** pl
bed	**postel** f	biscuit	**sušenka** f
bedroom	**ložnice** f	bishop	**biskup**
bee	**včela** f	a bit	**trochu**
before	**před**	to bite	**kousnout**
to begin	**začít**	bitter	**hořký**
beginner	**začátečník/**	black	**černý**
	začátečnice	black and white	**černobílý**
beginning	**začátek** m	black coffee	**černá káva** f
behind	**za**	blackcurrant	**černý rybíz** m
to believe (think)	**myslet**	blanket	**přikrývka** f
to believe (trust)	**věřit**	bleach	**bělicí**
bell	**zvonek** m		**prostředek** m
bell (church)	**zvon** m	to bleed	**krvácet**
to belong to	**patřit**	blind (eyes)	**slepý**
below	**pod**	blind (roller)	**roleta** f
belt	**pásek** m	blister	**puchýř** m
bend (in road)	**zatáčka** f	blocked	**ucpaný**
bent	**ohnutý**	blood	**krev** f
berth	**lůžko** n	blood pressure	**krevní tlak** m
beside	**vedle**	blouse	**halenka** f
best (the best)	**nejlepší**	blow-dry	**foukaná** f
better	**lepší**	blue	**modrý**
between	**mezi**	boarding	**nástup** m
bicycle	**kolo** n	boarding card	**palubní lístek** m
big	**velký**	boat	**loď** f
bigger	**větší**		

boat (motor) m	(motorový) člun
boat (steam)	parník
by boat	lodí
body	tělo n
bone	kost f
book	kniha f
booking	rezervace f
booking office	pokladna f/ (před)prodej m vstupenek
bookshop	knihkupectví n
boot (car)	kufr m auta
boots (Wellingtons)	gumové holínky
border	hranice f
boring	nudný
born	narozený
both (things)	oba m, obě f, obě n
bottle	láhev f
bottle opener	otvírač m na láhve
bottom	dno n
bow (decoration)	stuha f
bow tie	motýlek m
bowl	miska f
box	krabice f
box (theatre)	lóže f
box office	pokladna f/ (před)prodej m vstupenek
boy	chlapec

boyfriend: to have a boyfriend	chodit s někým
brain	mozek m
branch (office)	pobočka f
brand	značka f
brass	mosaz f
brave	odvážný
bread	chléb m
to break	zlomit
to break down	pokazit se
breakdown truck	odtahový vůz m
breakfast	snídaně f
to breathe	dýchat
bride	nevěsta
bridegroom	ženich
bridge	most m
briefcase	kufřík m, aktovka f
bright (colour)	zářivý
bright (clever)	bystrý
to bring	přinést
broad	široký
broken (not working)	pokažený
broken (leg)	zlomený
brother	bratr
brother-in-law	švagr
brown	hnědý
brown sugar	hnědý cukr m
bruise	modřina f
brush	kartáč m
to build	postavit

building	**budova** f
bulb (electric)	**žárovka** f
bull	**býk** m
burn (skin)	**popálenina** f
to burn	**hořet**
to burn smthg	**pálit**
to burn oneself	**spálit se**
bus	**autobus** m
by bus	**autobusem**
bush	**keř** m
business	**obchod** m
business studies	**studium** n **ekonomiky a obchodu**
business trip	**služební cesta** f
bus station	**autobusové nádraží** n
bus stop	**autobusová zastávka** f
busy (road)	**rušný**
I am busy	**mám moc práce**
but	**ale**
butane gas	**propanbutan** m
butcher's	**řeznictví** n
butter	**máslo** n
butterfly	**motýl** m
button	**knoflík** m
to buy	**koupit**

C

cabbage	**zelí** n
cabin (log)	**chata** f
café	**kavárna** f
call (telephone)	**hovor** m
to call (phone)	**telefonovat**
to make a call	**zatelefonovat si**
to call (visit)	**navštívit**
to be called	**jmenovat se**
calm	**klidný**
camera	**fotoaparát** m
to camp	**stanovat**
campbed	**skládací lůžko** n
campsite	**kemp/kemping** m
can (be able to)	**moci**
can (to know how to)	**umět**
can/tin	**konzerva** f
cancel	**zrušit**
can opener	**otvírák** m **na konzervy**
to cancel	**zrušit**
cancer	**rakovina** f
candle	**svíčka** f
canoe	**kánoe** ž
capital city	**hlavní město** n
car	**auto** n
by car	**autem**
caravan	**obytný přívěs** m
caravan site	**autokemping** m
cardigan	**svetr** m
care	**péče** f
care: to take care	**dávat pozor**

careful	**opatrný**
careless	**neopatrný**
car park	**parkoviště** n
carpenter	**tesař**
carpet	**koberec** m
carriage (railway)	**vůz** m/**vagón** m
carrot	**mrkev** f
to carry	**nést**
car wash	**mycí linka** f
case: just in case	**pro každý případ**
cash	**peníze** pl
cash: to pay by cash	**platit hotově**
to cash	**nechat proplatit**
cash desk/cashier	**pokladna** f
castle	**hrad** m
cat	**kočka** f
to catch	**chytit**
cauliflower	**květák** m
to cause	**způsobit**
cave	**jeskyně** f
ceiling	**strop** m
celeriac	**celer** m
cemetery	**hřbitov** m
central heating	**ústřední topení** n
century	**století** n
cereal	**obilné lupínky** pl
certain	**jistý**
certainly	**jistě**
certificate	**osvědčení** n
chain	**řetěz** m

chair	**židle** f
chairlift	**sedačková lanovka** f
change (coins)	**drobné** pl
to change	**vyměnit**
to change (clothes)	**převléct se**
to change (trains)	**přestupovat**
changing room	**šatna** f
chapel	**kaple** f
charge	**poplatek** m
charter flight	**speciál** m/**charterový let** m
cheap	**levný**
to check	**zkontrolovat**
check-in (desk)	**odbavení** n
to check in	**přihlásit se k odbavení**
cheek	**tvář** f
cheeky	**drzý**
Cheers!	**Na zdraví!**
cheese	**sýr** m
cherries	**třešně**
chess	**šachy** pl
chestnut	**kaštan** m
chewing gum	**žvýkačka** f
chicken	**kuře** n
chickenpox	**plané neštovice** pl
child	**dítě** n
children	**děti**
chimney	**komín** m
china	**porcelán** m

chips	**hranolky**	climber	**horolezec/**
chocolate	**čokoláda** f		**horolezkyně**
chocolates (box of)	**bonboniéra** f	climbing	**horolezectví** n
to choose	**vybrat si**	cloakroom	**šatna** f
chop (meat)	**kotleta** f	clock	**hodiny** pl
Christian	**křesťan/**	close (near)	**blízko**
	křesťanka	to close	**zavřít**
Christian name	**křestní jméno**	closed	**zavřeno**
Christmas	**vánoce** pl	cloth (for cleaning)	**hadr** m
Christmas Eve	**Štědrý den** m	clothing	**oblečení** n
Christmas Day	**Boží hod** m	cloud	**oblak** m
	vánoční	cloudy (adv.)	**oblačno**
church	**kostel** m	coach (bus)	**dálkový**
cigar	**doutník** m		**autobus** m
cigarette	**cigareta** f	coach (railway)	**vůz** m/**vagón** m
cigarette lighter	**zapalovač** m	coal	**uhlí** n
cinema	**kino** n	coarse	**hrubý**
circle	**kruh** m	coat	**kabát** m
circle (theatre)	**první pořadí**	coat hanger	**ramínko** n
city	**(velko)město** n	coin	**mince** f
civil servant	**státní úředník/**	cold	**studený**
	úřednice	I'm cold	**Je mi zima**
clean	**čistý**	It's cold	**Je chladno**
to clean	**čistit**	I've got a cold	**Mám rýmu**
cleansing milk	**pleťové mléko** n	collar	**límec** m
clear	**jasný**	colleague	**kolega/kolegyně**
clerk	**úředník/úřednice**	to collect	**sbírat**
clever	**chytrý**	collection (e.g.art)	**sbírka** f
cliff	**skalní stěna** f	collection (rubbish)	**odvoz** m **odpadků**
climate	**podnebí** n	college (further education)	**střední škola** f
to climb	**šplhat**		

college (higher education)	**vysoká škola** f
colour blind	**barvoslepý**
comb	**hřeben** m
to come	**přijít**
to come back	**vrátit se**
to come in	**vstoupit**
Come in!	**dále !**
comfortable	**pohodlný**
common (usual)	**obvyklý**
common (shared)	**společný**
company	**společnost** f
compared with	**v porovnání s**
compartment (train)	**kupé** n
to complain	**stěžovat si**
make a complaint	**reklamovat**
completely	**úplně**
complicated	**složitý**
compulsory	**povinný**
computer science	**nauka** f **o počítačích**
concert hall	**koncertní síň** f
concussion	**otřes** m **mozku**
condition (stipulation)	**podmínka** f
condition (state)	**stav** m
conditioner (hair)	**vlasový regenerátor** m
conductor	**průvodčí**
to confirm	**potvrdit**
conjunctivitis	**zánět** m **spojivek**

connection (travel)	**spoj** m
conscious	**při vědomí**
conservation	**ochrana** f **přírody**
constipation	**zácpa** f
to contact	**kontaktovat**
contact lenses	**kontaktní čočky**
contraceptive	**antikoncepce** f
convenient	**vyhovující**
cook	**kuchař/kuchařka**
cooker	**vařič** m/**sporák** m
cool	**chladný**
copper (metal)	**měď** f
copy	**kopie** f
to copy	**kopírovat**
cork	**korek** m
corner (outside)	**roh** m
correct	**správný**
corridor	**chodba** f
to cost: how much does it cost?	**kolik to stojí?**
cot	**dětská postýlka** f
cottage	**chalupa** f
cotton (material)	**bavlna** f
cotton (thread)	**nit** f
cotton wool	**vata** f
cough	**kašel** m
cough medicine	**něco proti kašli**
to count	**počítat**
counter (post office)	**přepážka** f
country	**země** f

countryside	**venkov** m
couple (people)	**pár** m
courgette	**cukína** f
course (lessons)	**kurz** m
course (meal)	**chod** m
court (law)	**soud** m
court (tennis)	**kurt** m
court(yard)	**nádvoří** n
cousin (male)/	**bratranec/**
(female)	**sestřenice**
cover charge	**kuvert** (slang) m
cow	**kráva** f
cramp (medical)	**křeč** f
crash (car)	**havárie** f
crayon	**pastelka** f
crazy	**bláznivý**
cream (cosmetics)	**krém** m
crisps	**brambůrky**
cross	**kříž** m
to cross (on foot)	**přejít**
to cross (in a vehicle)	**projet**
crossing (sea)	**přeplavba** f
crossroads	**křižovatka** f
crowded	**plný lidí**
crown	**koruna** f
cruise	**cesta** f **lodí**
to cry (weep)	**plakat**
crystal	**křišťál** m
cucumber	**okurka** f
cuisine	**kuchyně** f

cup	**šálek** m
cupboard	**skříň** f
cure (remedy)	**lék** m
to cure	**vyléčit**
current (electricity)	**proud** m
curtain (thin)	**záclona** f
curtain (heavy)	**závěs** m
curve (road)	**zatáčka** f
cushion	**polštářek** m
custard	**vanilkový krém** m
customs (office)	**celnice** f
customs (traditions)	**zvyky**
to cut	**řezat**
cutlery	**příbor** m sg
cycling	**cyklistika** f
cyclist	**cyklista/cyklistka**
cystitis	**zánět** m **močového měchýře**

D

daily	**denně**
damaged	**poškozený**
damp	**vlhký**
dance	**tanec** m
to dance	**tancovat**
danger	**nebezpečí** n
dangerous	**nebezpečný**
dark	**tmavý**
darling	**miláček** m/f

darts	šipky	degree (temperature)	stupeň *m*
data	údaje *pl*	degree (university)	vysokoškolský diplom *m*
date (day)	datum *n*		
date (fruit)	datle *f*	delay	zpoždění *n*
date (meeting)	schůzka *f*	delicious (taste)	vynikající
daughter	dcera	to deliver (letter)	doručit
daughter-in-law	snacha	dentures	umělý chrup *m sg*
day	den *m*	to depart (on foot)	odejít
day after tomorrow	pozítří	to depart (by road)	odjet
day before yesterday	předevčírem včera	to depart (by plane)	odletět
dead	mrtvý	department	oddělení *n*
deaf	hluchý	department store	obchodní dům *m*
dealer	obchodník/ obchodnice	departure (by road)	odjezd *m*
dear (expensive)	drahý	departure (by plane)	odlet *m*
death	smrt *f*		
debt	dluh *m*	departure lounge (airport)	odjezdová hala *f* odletová hala *f*
decaffeinated	bezkofeinový		
to decide	rozhodnout se	deposit (part payment)	záloha *f*
deck (ship)	paluba *f*		
deckchair	rozkládací lehátko *n*	to describe	popsat
		description	popis *m*
declare (customs): to have smthg to declare	mít něco k proclení	design (plan)	projekt *m*
		designer	projektant/ projektantka
deep	hluboký	dessert	dezert *m*
deep freeze	mraznička *f*	destination (travel)	cíl *m* cesty
deer	jelen *m*	detergent	prášek *m* na praní
defect	vada *f*		
definitely	rozhodně	to develop	rozvíjet
to defrost	odmrazit	to develop (a film)	vyvolat

diabetes	**cukrovka** f	dislocated	**vykloubený**
to dial	**vytočit**	disposable nappies	**pleny na jedno použití**
dialling code	**volací kód** m		
dialling tone	**oznamovací tón** m	distance	**vzdálenost** f
		distilled water	**destilovaná voda** f
diamond	**diamant** m		
diaper	**plenka** f	district (city)	**obvod** m
diarrhoea	**průjem** m	to dive	**skákat do vody**
diary	**deník** m	diversion (road)	**objížďka** f
dictionary	**slovník** m	diving board	**skákací prkno** n
to die	**zemřít**	divorced	**rozvedený**
He/She died	**zemřel** (he)/ **zemřela** (she)	dizzy: feel dizzy	**mít závrať**
		to do	**dělat**
diesel	**(motorová) nafta** f	doctor	**doktor/doktorka, lékař/lékařka**
diet	**dieta** f		
different	**jiný**	dog	**pes** m
difficult	**těžký**	doll	**panenka** f
difficulty	**problém** m	dome	**kupole** f
dining room	**jídelna** f	door	**dveře** pl
dinner	**večeře** f	double	**dvojitý**
direct	**přímý**	double bed	**dvoulůžko** n
direction	**směr** m	dough	**těsto** n
directory (telephone)	**telefonní seznam** m	down (direction)	**dolů**
		downstairs (ground floor)	**přízemí** n
dirty	**špinavý**		
disabled	**tělesně postižený**	draught	**sucho** n
disappointed	**zklamaný**	to draw (a picture)	**kreslit**
discount	**sleva** f	drawer (in chest of drawers)	**zásuvka** f
dish	**jídlo** n		
dishwasher	**myčka** f **na nádobí**	drawing	**kresba** f
		drawing pin	**napínáček** m
disinfectant	**dezinfekce** f	dreadful	**hrozný**

dress	**šaty** pl
dressing (medical)	**obvaz** m
dressing (salad)	**zálivka** f
drink	**nápoj** m
to drink	**pít**
to drip	**kapat**
to drive	**řídit**
driver	**řidič/řidička**
driving licence	**řidičský průkaz** m
drop	**kapka** n
drowned	**utopený**
drug (medicine)	**lék** m
drug (narcotic)	**droga** f
drug addict	**narkoman/ narkomanka**
drum	**buben** m
drunk	**opilý**
dry (weather)	**suchý**
dry cleaner	**chemická čistírna** f
dubbed (film)	**dabovaný**
duck (bird)	**kachna** f
dull (weather)	**pošmourný**
dull (knife)	**tupý**
dumb	**němý**
dummy (baby's)	**dudlík** m
during	**během**
dust	**prach** m
dusty	**prašný**
duty (customs)	**clo** n
duty-free	**bez cla**
duty-free shop	**obchod** m **s bezcelním zbožím/fríšop** m (slang)
duvet	**přikrývka** f

E

each	**každý**
ear	**ucho** n
earache: I have earache	**bolí mě ucho**
ear drops	**ušní kapky**
earlier	**dřív**
early	**časně**
to earn	**vydělávat**
earring	**náušnice** f
earth	**země** f
east	**východ** m
eastern	**východní**
Easter	**velikonoce** pl
easy	**snadný**
to eat	**jíst**
economical	**hospodárný**
either ... or ...	**buď ... nebo ...**
elastic	**guma** f
elastic bandage	**pružný obvaz** m
election	**volby** pl
electric	**elektrický**
electrician	**elektrikář**
else: something else	**něco jiného**
embarrassing	**trapný**

153

embassy	velvyslanectví n	estimate (cost)	odhad m
emergency	naléhavý případ m	evaporated milk	kondenzované mléko n
emergency exit	nouzový východ m	even (even faster)	dokonce
empty	prázdný	even (not odd)	sudý
to empty	vyprázdnit	evening	večer m
enamel	smalt m	evening dress	večerní šaty pl
end	konec m	every (each)	každý
to end	skončit	every (all)	všechny
engaged (occupied)	obsazeno	everyone	každý/všichni
		everything	všechno
engaged (to be married)	zasnoubený	everywhere	všude
		exactly	přesně
engine	motor m	examination (education)	zkouška f
engineer	technik/ technička	examination (medical)	vyšetření n
enough: that's enough	to stačí	example	příklad m
		for example	například
to enjoy oneself	bavit se	excellent	výborný
to enter	vstoupit	except	kromě
entertainment	zábava f	excess baggage	nadměrná váha f zavazadel
entrance	vchod m		
envelope	obálka f	to exchange	vyměnit
environment	životní prostředí n	exchange rate	směnný kurs m
		excited	vzrušený
equal	rovnoprávný	exciting	vzrušující
equipment	vybavení n	excursion	výlet m
escalator	eskalátor m	Excuse me	promiňte
especially	zvláště	executive (power)	výkonný
essential	velmi důležitý	exercise	cvičení n
estate (residential area)	sídliště n	exhibition	výstava f

exit	**východ** m	in fact	**vlastně**
to expect	**očekávat**	factory	**továrna** f
expenses	**výlohy** pl	to fail (exam)	**neudělat**
expensive	**drahý**	failure	**neúspěch** m
experience (skills)	**zkušenosti** pl	faint: he/she fainted	**omdlel** (male)/ **omdlela** (female)
experience (what happens to one)	**zážitek** m	fair (village f.)	**trh** m
to explain	**vysvětlit**	fair (hair)	**světlý**
extension (electric)	**prodlužovačka** f	fair (trade)	**veletrh** m
		fairly (quite)	**dost**
extension (phone number)	**linka** f	faith	**víra** f
external	**vnější**	faithful	**věrný**
extra (in addition)	**navíc**	fake	**falzifikát** m
eye	**oko** n	to fall	**upadnout**
eyebrow	**obočí** n	He/She had a fall	**Upadl** (male)/ **Upadla** (female)
eye drops	**oční kapky**	false (untrue)	**lživý**
eyelash	**řasa** f	false (teeth)	**falešný**
eye-liner	**tužka** f **na oční linky**	family	**rodina** f
		famous	**slavný**
eye-shadow	**oční stíny**	fan (supporter)	**fanoušek/fanyka**
eyesight	**zrak** m	fan (electric)	**větrák** m
		far (away)	**daleko**

F

		fare	**jízdné** n
fabric (textile)	**látka** f	farm	**farma** f
face	**obličej** m	farmer	**zemědělec** m
face cream	**krém** m **na obličej**	fashion	**móda** f
		fashionable	**módní**
face powder	**pudr** m	fast	**rychlý**
facilities (not toilets)	**vybavení** n	fat (meat)	**tuk** m
fact	**fakt** m	fat (adj.)	**tlustý**

father	**otec**
father-in-law	**tchán**
fault	**vada** f
faulty	**vadný**
favourite	**oblíbený**
feather	**pírko** n
fed up: I'm fed up	**mám toho dost**
fee	**poplatek** m
to feed	**krmit**
to feel	**cítit**
I feel well/ill	**cítím se dobře/ špatně**
felt-tip pen	**fix** m
female	**žena**
feminine (gender)	**ženský**
feminine (womanly)	**ženský**
fence	**plot** m
ferry	**trajekt** m
fever	**horečka** f
few	**málo**
a few	**několik**
fiancée	**snoubenec**(male)/ **snoubenka** (female)
fibre	**vlákno** n
field	**pole** n
fight (struggle)	**boj** m
fight (quarrel)	**hádka** f
file (office)	**složka** f
file (nail or DIY)	**pilník** m
filling (tooth)	**plomba** f

filling (food)	**sytirý**
film star	**filmová hvězda** f
to find	**najít**
fine (all right)	**dobře**
fine (weather)	**hezký**
fine (penalty)	**pokuta** f
finger	**prst** m
to finish	**skončit**
fire (flame)	**oheň** m
fire (on fire)	**hoří**
fire brigade	**hasiči** pl
fire extinguisher	**hasicí přístroj** m
firewood	**dřevo** n **na topení**
fireworks	**ohňostroj** m
firm (company)	**firma** f
first	**první**
first aid	**první pomoc** f
first aid kit	**příruční lékárnička** f
first class	**první třída** f
first name	**křestní jméno** n
fish	**ryba** f
to go fishing	**jít na ryby**
fishing	**rybaření** n
fishing rod	**rybářská udice** f
fishmonger	**obchod** m **s rybami**
fit (healthy)	**fit**
to fit (clothes)	**padnout**
fitting room	**zkušební kabina** f
to fix	**opravit**

fizzy	**šumivý**
flag	**vlajka** f
flash (photography)	**blesk** m
flat (apartment)	**byt** m
flat (level)	**rovný**
flat battery	**vybitá baterie** f
flat tyre	**píchlá pneumatika** f
flavour	**chuť** f, **příchuť** f
flaw	**chyba** f
flea	**blecha** f
flea market	**bleší trh** m
flight	**let** m
flippers	**gumové ploutve**
flood	**záplava** f
floor	**podlaha** f
floor (storey)	**patro** n
flour	**mouka** f
flu	**chřipka** f
fluid	**tekutina** f
fly	**moucha** f
foam	**pěna** f
fog	**mlha** f
foggy: it is foggy	**je mlha**
folding (chair, etc.)	**skládací**
folk (music)	**lidový**
to follow	**sledovat**
following (next)	**následující**
food	**potraviny** pl
food poisoning	**otrava** f **z jídla**
foot	**chodidlo** n

on foot	**pěšky**
football	**fotbal** m
footpath	**chodníček** m
for (preposition)	**pro**
forbidden	**zakázaný**
forecast (weather)	**předpověď** f
foreign	**zahraniční**
forest	**les** m
to forget	**zapomenout**
to forgive	**prominout**
fork	**vidlička** f
form (document)	**formulář** m
fortnight	**čtrnáct dní**
forward (direction)	**dopředu**
foundation (make-up)	**podkladový krém** m
fracture	**zlomenina** f
fragile	**křehký**
frame (glasses)	**obroučky** pl
frankly	**upřímně řečeno**
freckles	**pihy**
free (gratis): it's free	**zadarmo**
free (available, unoccupied)	**volný**
freedom	**svoboda** f
to freeze	**zmrazit**
freezer	**mraznička** f
frequent	**častý**
fresh	**čerstvý**
fridge	**lednička** f

fried	**smažený/ restovaný**	gambling	**hazardní hry** pl
friend	**přítel/přítelkyně**	game (sport or board)	**hra** f
frightened	**vylekaný**	game (match)	**utkání** n
fringe (hair)	**ofina** f	game (meat)	**zvěřina** f
frog	**žába** f	garden	**zahrada** f
from	**z/od**	gardener	**zahradník/ zahradnice**
front: in front of	**před**		
front door	**hlavní vchod** m	garlic	**česnek** m
frontier	**hranice** f	gas bottle	**plynová láhev** f
frost	**mráz** m	gastritis	**gastritida** f
frozen	**zmrazený**	gate	**brána** f
fruit	**ovoce** n	gauze	**gáza** f
frying pan	**pánev** f **na smažení**	general (military)	**generál**
		general (adj.)	**všeobecný**
fuel	**palivo** n	generous	**velkorysý**
full	**plný**	gentle	**jemný**
full board	**plná penze** f	gentleman	**pán**
full up (booked up)	**vyprodaný**	genuine	**pravý**
funeral	**pohřeb** m	to get (obtain)	**dostat**
funfair	**pouť** f	to get off	**vystoupit**
funny (amusing)	**zábavný**	to get on	**nastoupit**
funny (peculiar)	**divný**	gift (present)	**dárek** m
fur	**kožešina** f	girl	**dívka**
furniture	**nábytek** m	girlfriend	**přítelkyně**
further on	**dál**	to give	**dát**
fuse	**pojistka** f	glass	**sklenice** f
fuse box	**pojistky** pl	glass (material)	**sklo** n
		glasses (spectacles)	**brýle** pl
		glove	**rukavice** f
		glue	**lepidlo** n

G

gallery	**galerie** f

to go	**jít**
Let's go (on foot)	**Pojďme**
Let's go (by transport)	**Jeďme**
to go away	**odejít**
to go down	**sejít**
to go in	**vstoupit**
to go out	**vyjít ven**
to go up (on foot)	**vyjít (nahoru)**
to go up (by transport)	**vyjet (nahoru)**
goal (sport)	**gól** m
goal (aim)	**cíl** m
goat	**koza** f
God	**bůh** m
gold	**zlato** n
made of gold	**zlatý**
gold plated	**pozlacený**
golf course	**golfové hřiště** n
good	**dobrý**
good afternoon/ evening	**dobré odpoledne/ večer**
goodbye	**na shledanou**
good morning	**dobrý den**
good night	**dobrou noc**
government	**vláda** f
grammar	**gramatika** f
grandchildren	**vnoučata**
granddaughter	**vnučka**
grandfather	**dědeček**
grandmother	**babička**
grandparents	**prarodiče**

grandson	**vnuk**
grape	**hrozen** m
grapefruit	**grep** m
grass	**tráva** f
grateful	**vděčný**
greasy (covered in grease)	**mastný**
great	**velký**
Great!	**Skvělé!**
green	**zelený**
green card (insurance certificate)	**zelená karta** f
greengrocer's	**obchod** m s ovocem a zeleninou
to greet	**zdravit**
grey	**šedý**
grilled	**grilovaný**
grocer's	**obchod s potravinami**
ground (earth)	**zem** f
ground floor	**přízemí** n
groundsheet	**podlážka** n
group	**skupina** f
to grow	**růst**
guarantee	**záruka** f
guest	**host** m (no female form)
guest house	**penzion** m
guide	**průvodce/ průvodkyně**
guidebook	**průvodce** m

guided tour	prohlídka f s průvodcem	handicapped	tělesně postižený/ tělesně postižená
guilty	vinný		
guitar	kytara f	handkerchief	kapesník m
gun	revolver m	handle (door)	klika f
		handle (cup)	ucho n

H

		hand luggage	příruční zavazadlo n
habit (custom)	zvyk m	handmade	ručně vyrobený
haemorrhoids	hemeroidy	hangover	kocovina f
hail	kroupy pl	to hang (up)	zavěsit
hair	vlasy pl	to happen	stát se
hairbrush	kartáč m na vlasy	What's happened?	Co se stalo?
hair curlers	natáčky		
haircut: to have a haircut	dát se ostříhat	happy	šťastný
		hard (firm)	tvrdý
hairdresser's	kadeřnictví n	hard (difficult)	těžký
hair dryer	fén m	hat	klobouk m
hair grip	sponka f do vlasů	to hate	nenávidět
hair spray	lak m na vlasy	to have	mít
hair style	účes m	Do you have ...?	Máte...? (formal)
half	půl		Máš...? (informal)
(a) half	polovina f	hay fever	senná rýma f
half board	polopenze f	hazelnut	lískový ořech m
half-hour	půlhodina f	he	on
hall (in house)	předsíň f	head (body)	hlava f
hall (concert)	sál m	head (boss)	vedoucí m/f
hammer	kladivo n	head (school, etc.)	ředitel/ředitelka
hammock	houpací síť f	headache: I have a headache	bolí mě hlava
handbag	kabelka f		
hand cream	krém m na ruce	headphones	sluchátka

to heal	**zahojit se**	to have hiccoughs	**mít škytavku**
health	**zdraví** n	high	**vysoký**
health foods	**potraviny pro zdravou výživu**	highchair	**dětská židle** f
healthy	**zdravý**	to hijack	**unést**
to hear	**slyšet**	hill	**kopec** m
hearing aid	**naslouchátka** pl	him	**jemu, mu/, jeho/ho**
heart attack	**infarkt** m	for him	**pro něj**
heat	**horko** n	with/without him	**s ním/bez něj**
to heat	**topit**	to hire	**najmout si**
heater	**kamínka** pl/ **ohřívač** m	his (own)	**jeho**
		to hit	**udeřit**
heating	**topení** n	to hitch-hike	**stopovat**
heaven	**nebe** n	hole	**díra** f
heavy	**těžký**	holiday(s)	**dovolená** f
hedge	**živý plot** m	school holidays	**prázdniny** pl
heel (foot)	**pata** f	on holiday	**na dovolené/ na prázdninách**
heel (shoe)	**podpatek** m		
height	**výška** f	public holiday	**státní svátek** m
hell	**peklo** n	holy	**svatý**
hello	**dobrý den** (formal)/ **ahoj** (informal)	home	**domov** m
		at home	**doma**
help	**pomoc** f	to go home	**jít domů**
to help	**pomoci**	home address	**trvalé bydliště** n
her (own)	**její**	honest	**čestný**
for her	**pro ni**	honeymoon	**svatební cesta** f
with/without her	**s ní/bez ní**	to hope	**doufat**
herb	**bylina** f	I hope so	**to doufám**
here	**tady**	I hope not	**doufám, že ne**
hiccoughs	**škytavka** f	horrible	**hrozný**
		horse	**kůň** m

horse riding	jízda *f* na koni
hose	hadice *f*
hospital	nemocnice *f*
hot (temperature)	horký
I'm hot	Je mi horko
It's hot (weather)	Je horko
hot (spicy)	ostrý
hot water bottle	ohřívací láhev *f*
hotel directory	seznam *m* hotelů
hour	hodina *f*
house	dům *m*
housewife	žena v domácnosti
housework	domácí práce
how?	jak?
How are you?	Jak se máte? (formal) Jak se máš? (informal)
How far?	Jak daleko?
How long? (adv.)	Jak dlouho?
How many/much?	Kolik?
How much is it?	Kolik to stojí?
human	lidský
hungry	hladový
to be hungry	mít hlad
to hunt	lovit
hunting	lov *m*
hurry	spěch *m*
to be in a hurry	spěchat
to hurt (someone)	zranit
to hurt (my ... hurts)	bolet
husband	manžel
hut	chata *f*

I

I	já
ice	led *m*
ice cream	zmrzlina *f*
ice rink	kluziště *n*
icy	ledový
idea	nápad *m*
if	jestli
ill	nemocný
illness	nemoc *f*
to imagine	představit si
immediately	okamžitě
immersion heater	ponorný vařič *m*
impatient	netrpělivý
important	důležitý
impossible	nemožný
impressive	impozantní
in (a place)	v
included	zahrnutý
including	včetně
income	příjem *m*
independent	nezávislý
indigestion	špatné trávení *n*
indoor (swimming pool)	krytý
industrial	průmyslový

infected	**nakažený**
infection	**infekce** f
infectious	**nakažlivý**
inflamed (medical)	**zanícený**
inflammation	**zánět** m
influenza	**chřipka** f
informal	**neformální**
information office	**informační kancelář** f
injection	**injekce** f
injured	**poraněný**
injury	**poranění** n
ink	**inkoust** m
inner	**vnitřní**
innocent	**nevinný**
insect	**hmyz** m
insect bite	**bodnutí** n **hmyzem**
insecticide	**insekticid** m
insect repellent	**repelent** m **proti hmyzu**
inside	**uvnitř**
to insist (on)	**trvat (na)**
instant coffee	**instantní káva** f
instead of	**místo**
instructor	**instruktor/ instruktorka**
insult	**urážka** f
insurance	**pojištění** n
insurance certificate	**pojišťovací dokument** m

interested: I'm (not) interested (in)	**(ne)zajímám se (o)**
interesting	**zajímavý**
internal	**vnitřní**
international	**mezinárodní**
interpreter	**tlumočník/ tlumočnice**
interval (theatre)	**přestávka** f
interview	**rozhovor** m
into	**do**
to introduce	**představit**
to invite	**pozvat**
invitation	**pozvání** n
iodine	**jód** m
iron (metal)	**železo** n
iron (for clothes)	**žehlička** f
to iron	**žehlit**
ironmonger's	**železářství** n
is	**je**
He/She/It is	**On/Ona/Ono je**
island	**ostrov** m
it	**to**
to itch	**svědit**

J

jacket	**sako** n/**kabátek** m
jam	**džem** m/ **marmeláda** f
jar	**nádoba** f
jazz	**džez** m

jeans	**džíny**	kilometre	**kilometr** *m*
Jesus/Jesus Christ	**Ježíš/Ježíš Kristus**	kind (person)	**laskavý**
		That's very kind of you	**To je od vás moc hezké**
jelly	**želé** *n*	kind (sort)	**druh** *m*
jeweller's	**klenotnictví** *n*	king	**král**
Jewish (noun)	**žid/židovka**	kiss	**polibek** *m*
Jewish (adj.)	**židovský**	to kiss	**líbat**
job	**zaměstnání** *n*	kitchen	**kuchyň** *f*
jogging	**kondiční běh** *m*	knickers	**kalhotky**
to go jogging	**chodit běhat**	knife	**nůž** *m*
I go jogging	**chodím běhat**	to knit	**plést**
joke	**vtip** *m*	to knock	**klepat**
journalist	**novinář/ novinářka**	to knock down (by car, etc.)	**srazit**
journey	**cesta** *f*	knot	**uzel** *m*
judge	**soudce/ soudkyně**	to know (someone)	**znát**
jug	**džbánek** *m*	I don't know him/her	**neznám ho/ ji**
juice	**džus** *m*	to know (have knowledge of)	**vědět**
to jump	**skočit**	I (don't) know	**(ne)vím**
jumper	**svetr** *m*	to know how to	**umět**
junction (road)	**křižovatka** *f*	I (don't) know how to	**(ne)umím**
just (only)	**jen**		
just (now)	**právě**		

K

to keep	**nechat si**
kettle	**konvice** *f*
key	**klíč** *m*
to kill	**zabít**
kilo(gram)	**kilo** *n*

L

label	**nálepka** *f*
lace (cloth)	**krajka** *f*
lace (shoe)	**tkanička** *f*

ladder	**žebřík** m
lady	**dáma**
ladies and gentlemen	**dámy a pánové**
lake	**jezero** n
lamb (meat)	**jehněčí** n
lamp	**lampa** f
land	**země** f
to land	**přistát**
landlady	**bytná**
landlord	**bytný**
lane (on motorway)	**jízdní pruh** m
language	**jazyk** m
large	**velký**
last (the last)	**poslední**
last (the past)	**minulý**
to last	**trvat**
late	**pozdě**
It's late	**Je pozdě**
later	**později**
to laugh	**smát se**
laundry (place)	**prádelna** f
laundry (clothes)	**prádlo** n
law (act)	**zákon** m
to study law	**studovat práva**
lawyer	**právník/právnička**
laxative	**projímadlo** n
lazy	**líný**
to lead	**vést**
lead (metal)	**olovo** n
lead-free	**bezolovnatý**

leaf	**list** m
leaflet	**prospekt** m/ **leták** m
to leak (water)	**téct**
to leak (gas)	**unikat**
to learn	**učit se**
learner	**student/ studentka**
least: at least	**aspoň**
leather	**kůže** f
to leave (message, etc.)	**nechat**
to leave (to go away): on foot/ by transport	**odejít/ odjet**
left	**levý**
to the left	**doleva**
on the left	**vlevo**
left hand	**levá ruka** f
left-handed	**levák**
legal	**legální**
lemon	**citrón** m
lemonade (lemon drink)	**citronáda** f
to lend	**půjčit**
length	**délka** f
lens (in glasses)	**skla** pl
contact lenses	**kontaktní čočky**
less	**méně**
lesson	**lekce** f
to let (allow)	**nechat**
Let me know	**Dejte mi vědět**

to let (for rent)	**pronajmout**	like this/that	**takový**
(a house) to let	**k pronajmutí**	What ... like?	**Jaký?**
letter	**dopis** *m*	What is it like?	**Jaké to je?**
letter (of alphabet)	**písmeno** *n*	like: I like	**líbí se mi/(mám) rád** (male) **ráda** (female)
letterbox	**poštovní schránka** *f*		
level (height, standard)	**úroveň** *f*	I like the dress	**Líbí se mi ty šaty**
library	**knihovna** *f*	I like opera	**Mám ráda operu**
licence	**oprávnění** *n*	I like driving	**Rád/Ráda řídím**
licence (fishing, etc.)	**povolení** *n*	likely	**pravděpodobný**
		limited	**omezený**
driving licence	**řidičský průkaz** *m*	line	**linka** *f*
lid	**víko** *n*	linen: bed linen	**ložní prádlo** *n*
to lie down	**lehnout si**	lion	**lev**
life	**život** *m*	lipsalve	**pomáda** *f* **na rty**
lifebelt	**záchranný pás** *m*	lipstick	**rtěnka** *f*
lifeboat	**záchranný člun** *m*	liqueur	**likér** *m*
lifeguard (swimming pool)	**plavčík/plavčice**	liquid	**tekutina** *f*
		list	**seznam** *m*
lifejacket	**záchranná vesta** *f*	to listen	**poslouchat**
lift (elevator)	**výtah** *m*	litre	**litr** *m*
to lift	**zvednout**	litter (rubbish)	**odpadky** *pl*
light	**světlo** *n*	little (small)	**malý**
switch on a light	**rozsvítit**	a little	**trochu**
light (colour)	**světlý**	to live	**žít**
light (weight)	**lehký**	liver	**játra** *pl*
to light (fire, etc.)	**rozsvítit**	living room	**obývací pokoj** *m*
light bulb	**žárovka** *f*	loaf (of bread)	**bochník** *m*
lighter	**zapalovač** *m*	local	**místní**
lightning	**blesk** *m*	lock	**zámek** *m*
like (similar to)	**jako**	to lock	**zamknout**

lonely	**osamělý**
long (journey, etc.)	**dlouhý**
long (adv.)	**dlouho**
to look (at)	**dívat se (na)**
to look (after)	**starat se (o)**
to look (for)	**hledat**
to look (forward to)	**těšit se (na)**
to look (like)	**podobat se**
lorry	**nákladní auto** n
lorry driver	**řidič nákladního auta**
to lose	**ztratit**
loss	**ztráta** f
lost property office	**ztráty a nálezy**
a lot (of)	**spousta**
lotion (tonic)	**pleťová voda** f
loud	**hlasitý**
lounge (hotel)	**hala** f
love	**láska** f
to love	**mít rád/milovat** (stronger)
lovely	**hezký**
low	**nízký**
lower (adj.)	**spodní**
lozenge	**pastilka** f
luck	**štěstí** n
lucky: to be lucky	**mít štěstí**
luggage	**zavazadlo** n sg **zavazadla** pl
lump (medical)	**boule** f
lunch	**oběd** m

M

machine	**stroj** m
mad	**šílený**
magazine	**časopis** m
magnificent	**překrásný**
maid	**pokojská**
main	**hlavní**
make (brand)	**značka** f
male	**mužský**
man (male)	**muž**
man (human being)	**člověk** m
manager	**manažer/vedoucí**
manageress	**manažerka/vedoucí**
managing director	**ředitel/ředitelka**
many	**mnoho**
marble	**mramor** m
market	**trh** m
married (of a man)	**ženatý**
married (of a woman)	**vdaná**
mascara	**řasenka** f
mass (church)	**mše** f
match (sport)	**zápas** m
matches	**zápalky**
matter: it doesn't matter	**to nevadí**
What's the matter?	**Co se stalo?**
mattress	**matrace** f

mature	**zralý**
me	**mě, mně, mi**
for me	**pro mě**
with me/without me	**se mnou/beze mě**
meadow	**louka** f
meal	**jídlo** n
to mean	**znamenat**
What does it mean?	**Co to znamená?**
meanwhile	**mezitím**
measles	**spalničky**
German measles	**zarděnky**
to measure	**měřit**
measurement	**míra** f
meat	**maso** n
cold meats	**nářez** m
medicine (drug)	**lék** m
Mediterranean Sea	**Středozemní moře** n
medium-size	**středně velký**
meeting	**setkání** n **schůze** f
to meet	**setkat se**
member	**člen/členka**
to mend	**opravit**
message	**vzkaz** m
meter (taxi)	**taxametr** m
meter (parking)	**parkovací hodiny** pl
metre	**metr** m
microwave (oven)	**mikrovlnka** f
midday	**poledne** n

middle: in the middle	**uprostřed**
middle-aged	**středního věku**
midnight	**půlnoc** f
mild (taste)	**jemný**
mild (temperature)	**mírný**
mile	**míle** f
milk	**mléko** n
milk-shake	**mléčný koktejl** m
mill	**mlýnek** m
mince (meat)	**mleté maso** m
mind: do you mind if ...?	**Bude vám** (formal) **/ti** (informal) **vadit, když ... ?**
I don't mind	**Nevadí mi to**
Never mind	**To nevadí**
mine (of me)	**můj**
minister (in politics)	**ministr/ministryně**
minute (time)	**minuta** f
mirror	**zrcadlo** n
Miss	**slečna**
to miss (bus, etc.)	**nestihnout**
to miss (not to have)	**postrádat**
mist	**mlha** f
mistake	**chyba** f
mistaken: to be mistaken	**mýlit se**
mixed	**míchaný**
modern	**moderní**

moisturiser	**hydratační krém** m
monastery	**klášter** m
money	**peníze** pl
month	**měsíc** m
monument: historical monument	**památka** f
moon	**měsíc** m
more	**víc**
morning	**ráno** n
mortgage	**hypotéka** f
mosquito	**komár** m
most (of)	**většina**
mother	**matka**
mother-in-law	**tchýně**
motor	**motor** m
motorbike	**motorka** f
motorboat	**motorový člun** m
motor racing	**závody** pl **automobilů**
motorway	**dálnice** f
mountain	**hora** f
montaineering	**horolezectví** n
motorbike	**motorka** f
moustache	**knír** m
mouth	**ústa** pl
to move	**hýbat se**
movement	**pohyb** m
Mr	**pan**
Mrs	**paní**
much	**hodně**
not much	**moc ne**

mug	**hrnek** m
to murder	**zavraždit**
mushroom	**žampión** f
wild mushrooms	**houby**
music	**hudba** f
musician	**hudebník/ hudebnice**
must	**muset**
I must	**musím**
my	**můj**

N

nail	**hřebík** m
nail (finger/toe)	**nehet** m
nail file	**pilník** m **na nehty**
nail polish	**lak** m **na nehty**
nail polish remover	**odlakovač** m
naked	**nahý**
name	**jméno** n
first name	**křestní jméno** n
My name is ...	**Jmenuju se ...**
What's your name?	**Jak se jmenujete?** (formal)/**Jak se jmenuješ?** (informal)
napkin	**ubrousek** m
nappy	**plenka** f
narrow	**úzký**
national	**národní**
nationality	**národnost** f

naughty	**zlobivý**
navy-blue	**námořnická modř** f
near (to)	**blízko**
nearly	**téměř**
necessary	**nutný**
necklace/chain	**náhrdelník** m/ **řetízek** m
to need	**potřebovat**
needle	**jehla** f
negative (photo)	**negativ** m
neighbour	**soused/ sousedka**
neither ... nor ...	**ani ... ani ...**
nephew	**synovec**
nervous	**nervózní**
net	**síť** f
never	**nikdy**
new	**nový**
New Year	**Nový rok** m
news (TV/radio)	**zprávy** pl
newspaper	**noviny** pl
next	**příští**
nice (person)	**milý**
nice (place, etc.)	**hezký**
niece	**neteř**
night	**noc** f
at night	**v noci**
nightdress	**noční košile** f
no	**ne**
nobody	**nikdo**
noise	**hluk** m

noisy	**hlučný**
non-alcoholic	**nealkoholický**
non-smoking	**nekuřácký**
normal	**normální**
north	**sever** m
northern	**severní**
nose	**nos** m
nosebleed	**krvácení** n **z nosu**
not	**ne, ne-** (with a verb)
note (bank)	**bankovka** f
notepad	**blok** m
nothing	**nic**
notice (sign)	**nápis** m
to notify	**informovat**
now	**teď**
nowhere	**nikde**
nuclear	**jaderný**
nuclear energy	**jaderná energie** f
number	**číslo** n
nurse	**sestra** f **ošetřovatel** m
nut	**ořech** m
nut (for bolt)	**matice** f

O

oar	**veslo** n
object	**předmět** m
obvious	**evidentní**
occasionally	**příležitostně**
occupation	**zaměstnání** n

occupied (seat)	**obsazený**
o'clock	**hodin**
odd (peculiar)	**zvláštní**
odd (not even)	**lichý**
of course	**ovšem**
off (switched off)	**vypnutý**
offended	**uražený**
office (a room)	**kancelář** f
office (institution)	**úřad** m
often	**často**
How often?	**Jak často?**
oil (car, cooking)	**olej** m
oily (greasy)	**mastný**
OK	**v pořádku/dobrá**
old	**starý**
How old are you?	**Kolik je vám let?** (formal)/ **Kolik je ti let?** (informal)
I'm ... years old	**Je mi ... let**
old-fashioned	**staromódní**
olive	**oliva** f
olive oil	**olivový olej** m
on	**na**
switched on	**zapnutý**
once (one time)	**jednou**
at once	**hned**
onion	**cibule** f
only	**jen**
open	**otevřený**
to open	**otevřít**

opera/opera house	**opera** f
operation	**operace** f
opinion	**názor** m
in my opinion	**podle mého názoru**
opposite (contrary)	**opačný**
opposite (on the other side)	**naproti**
optician's	**optika** f
or	**nebo**
orange (fruit)	**pomeranč** m
orange (colour)	**oranžový**
to order (to ask for)	**objednat**
ordinary	**obyčejný**
to organise	**organizovat**
other	**jiný**
others	**jiní**
our, ours	**náš**
out: he/she is out	**není tu**
outdoors	**pod širým nebem**
outside	**venku**
over (above)	**nad**
to overtake	**předjet**
owner	**majitel/majitelka**

P

package	**balík** m
package tour	**zájezd** m

171

packet (of cigarettes)	**krabička** f	passport	**pas** m
padlock	**visací zámek** m	past	**minulost** f
page	**stránka** f	in the past	**v minulosti**
pain	**bolest** f	path	**pěšina** f
painful	**bolestivý**	patient	**trpělivý**
painkiller	**prášek** m **proti bolesti**	patient (medical)	**pacient/pacientka**
paint	**barva** f	pattern (fabric, etc.)	**vzor** m
to paint (pictures)	**malovat**	pavement	**chodník** m
painter	**malíř/malířka**	to pay	**platit**
painting	**obraz** m	to pay cash	**platit hotově**
pair	**pár** m	peace	**mír** m
palace	**palác** m	peach	**broskev** f
pale (of face)	**bledý**	peanut	**burák** m
pale (colour)	**světlý**	pear	**hruška** f
pants (underwear):		peas	**hrášek** m sg
men's	**spodky** pl	pedal	**pedál** m
women's	**kalhotky** pl	pedestrian	**chodec** (only male form)
paper	**papír** m		
parcel	**balík** m	pedestrian crossing	**přechod** m **pro chodce**
parents	**rodiče**		
to park	**parkovat**	to peel	**oloupat**
parking	**parkování** n	peg (tent)	**kolík** m
parliament	**parlament** m	pen	**pero** n
part	**část** f	pencil	**tužka** f
parting (hair)	**pěšinka** f	pencil sharpener	**ořezávátko** n
partly	**částečně**	pendant	**přívěšek** m
party (celebration)	**párty** f/**oslava** f	penfriend: to have a penfriend	**dopisovat si s někým**
to pass (salt, etc.)	**podat**	penknife	**kapesní nůž** m
to pass (exam)	**udělat zkoušku**	pension (old age)	**penze** f
passenger	**cestující** m/f	people	**lidé**

pepper (seasoning)	**pepř** m
pepper (vegetable)	**paprika** f
peppermint	**máta** f
peppermint tea	**mátový čaj** m
per	**za**
per cent	**procento** n
per person per day	**za osobu a den**
perfect	**perfektní**
performance (theatre)	**představení** n
perhaps	**snad**
period (menstrual)	**menstruace** f
period pains	**menstruační bolesti**
perm	**trvalá** f
permit	**povolení** m
to permit	**povolit**
person	**osoba** f
personal	**osobní**
personal stereo	**walkman** m
petrol	**benzín** m
petrol can	**benzínový kanistr** m
petrol station	**benzínová stanice** f
pharmacy	**lékárna** f
photo	**fotka** f
to photocopy	**oxeroxovat**
phrase book	**konverzační příručka** f

physics	**fyzika** f
piano	**piáno** n
to pick (choose)	**vybrat si**
to pick (flowers, etc.)	**trhat**
pickpocket	**kapesní zloděj**
picture	**obraz** m (larger) **obrázek** m (smaller)
piece	**kus** m
pig	**vepř** m
pill	**pilulka** f
Pill (contraceptive)	**antikoncepce** f
pillow	**polštář** m
pillowcase	**povlak** m **na polštář**
pin	**špendlík** m
pineapple	**ananas** m
pink	**růžový**
pipe (smoking)	**dýmka** f
pipe (drain, etc.)	**potrubí** n
place	**místo** n
plane (aeroplane)	**letadlo** n
by plane	**letadlem**
plant	**rostlina** f
plaster (sticking)	**náplast** f
plaster cast	**sádra** f
plastic bag	**igelitová taška** f
plate	**talíř** m
platform (station)	**nástupiště** n
play (theatre)	**hra** f

to play (instrument)	**hrát (na)**	portable	**přenosný**
		porter	**vrátný/vrátná**
to play (sport)	**hrát**	hotel porter	**portýr**
pleasant	**příjemný**	luggage porter	**nosič**
please	**prosím**	possible	**možný**
pleased	**potěšen**	as soon as possible	**co nejdříve**
plenty	**spousta**		
pliers	**kleště**	if possible	**pokud možno**
plimsolls	**tenisky**	possibly	**možná**
plug (bath)	**zátka** f	post (mail)	**pošta** f
plug (electrical)	**zástrčka** f	to post	**odeslat**
plumber	**instalatér**	postbox	**poštovní schránka** f
pneumonia	**zápal** m **plic**		
pocket	**kapsa** f	postcard	**pohlednice** f
point	**bod** m	postcode	**poštovní směrovací číslo** n
two point five	**dvě celé pět**		
poisoning	**otrava** f	poster	**plakát** m
poisonous	**jedovatý**	postman	**pošťák/pošťačka**
police station	**policejní stanice** f	post office	**pošta** f
polite	**zdvořilý**	to postpone	**odložit**
political	**politický**	pot (cooking)	**hrnec** m
politician	**politik/politička**	potatoes	**brambory**
politics	**politika** f	pottery (products)	**keramika** f
polluted	**znečištěný**	potty (child's)	**nočník** m
pollution	**znečištění** n	pound (sterling)	**anglická libra** f
pool (swimming)	**bazén** m	to pour	**lít**
poor	**chudý**	powder	**prášek** m
Pope	**papež**	powder (talc)	**pudr** m
popular	**populární**	power	**moc** f
pork	**vepřové** n	power (electrical)	**proud** m
port	**přístav** m	power cut	**přerušení** n **proudu**

pram	kočárek m	to pump up	napumpovat
to prefer	dávat přednost/ preferovat	puncture	píchlá pneumatika f
pregnant	těhotná	pure	čistý
to prepare	připravit	purple	fialový
prescription	předpis m	purse	peněženka f
present	dárek m	purse (US)	kabelka f
pretty	hezký	to push	tlačit
price	cena f	push-chair	skládací kočárek m
priest	kněz m	to put down	položit
prime minister	premiér/ premiérka	to put on	obléct si
prince	princ	pyjamas	pyžamo n sg
princess	princezna		

Q

quality	kvalita f
quarter	čtvrtina f
quarter (town)	čtvrť f
quay	nábřeží n
queen	královna
question	otázka f
queue	fronta f
quick	rychlý
quickly	rychle
quiet	tichý
quite (fairly)	docela
quite (completely)	velmi

print (photo)	fotka f
print (picture)	reprodukce f
prison	vězení n
private	soukromý
prize	cena f
probably	pravděpodobně
profession	profese f
profit	zisk m
programme	program m
prohibited	zakázaný
promise	slib m
to pronounce	vyslovovat
pronunciation	výslovnost
properly	patřičně
public	veřejný
public holiday	státní svátek m
to pull	táhnout

R

rabbit	králík m
rabies	vzteklina f

race (sport)	**závod** m
racecourse/track	**závodní dráha** f
racecourse (horses)	**dostihová dráha** f
racing (horse)	**dostihy** pl
racing (motor)	**závody** pl
racket (tennis, etc.)	**raketa** f
radio station	**rozhlasová stanice** f
railway	**železnice** f
railway station	**nádraží** n
rain	**déšť** m
to rain	**pršet**
It's raining	**Prší**
raincoat	**pláštěnka** f/ **nepromokavý plášť** m
rainy	**deštivý**
to rape	**znásilnit**
rare (infrequent)	**vzácný**
rare (steak)	**krvavý**
rash (on skin)	**vyrážka** f
raspberries	**maliny**
rate (speed)	**tempo** n
rate (tariff)	**sazba** f
rather (quite)	**dost**
raw	**syrový**
razor (electrical)	**holicí strojek** m
razor blades	**žiletky**
to reach (on foot)	**dojít**
to reach (by transport)	**dojet**

to read	**číst**
reading	**četba** f
ready	**hotový**
real (authentic)	**pravý**
really	**opravdu**
rear	**zadní**
reason	**důvod** m
the reason why	**důvod proč**
receipt	**účtenka** f/ **paragon** m
to recognise	**uznat**
to recommend	**doporučit**
record (music)	**gramofonová deska** f
to record	**nahrát**
red	**červený**
Red Cross	**červený kříž** m
to refill	**doplnit**
refill (pen)	**náhradní náplň** f
refrigerator	**lednička** f
to refund	**proplatit**
region	**oblast** f
to register (oneself)	**zaregistrovat se**
to register (letter)	**poslat doporučeně**
registration number	**státní poznávací značka** f
relation	**příbuzný/ příbuzná**
religion	**náboženství** n
to remain	**zůstat**
to remember	**pamatovat si**

I can't remember	**Nemohu si vzpomenout**
to rent	**najmout si**
rent (money to pay)	**nájemné** n
to repair	**opravit**
to repeat	**opakovat**
reply	**odpověď** f
report (business, etc.)	**zpráva** f
to report	**hlásit**
to rescue	**zachránit**
reservation (booking)	**rezervace** f
reservation (complaint)	**výhrada** f
to reserve	**rezervovat si**
reserved (table)	**rezervovaný**
responsible	**odpovědný**
rest (remaining)	**zbytek** m
to rest	**odpočinout si**
restaurant car	**jídelní vůz** m
result	**výsledek** m
retired	**v důchodu**
return	**návrat** m
return (ticket)	**zpáteční**
to return (give back)	**vrátit**
to return (oneself)	**vrátit se**
reverse charge call	**hovor** m **na účet volaného**
rice	**rýže** f
rich	**bohatý**
to ride (a bike/ in a car)	**jezdit (na kole/ autem)**
to ride a horse	**jezdit na koni**
right	**pravý**
on the right	**vpravo**
to the right	**doprava**
right: you are right	**máš** (informal)/ **máte** (formal) **pravdu**
That's right	**To je pravda/ Správně**
right-hand side	**pravá strana** f
on the right-hand side	**na pravé straně**
ring (jewellery)	**prsten** m
ripe	**zralý**
river	**řeka** f
road	**silnice** f
to rob	**okrást**
I've been robbed	**okradli mě**
robbery	**krádež** f
roof	**střecha** f
room (house)	**místnost** f
room (space)	**prostor** m
rope	**lano** n
rose	**růže** f
rotten	**shnilý**
rough (surface)	**drsný**
round	**kulatý**
roundabout (funfair)	**kolotoč** m
roundabout (traffic)	**kruhový objezd** m

route	**trasa** f
row (theatre, etc.)	**řada** f
to row	**veslovat**
rowing boat	**veslovací loďka** f
royal	**královský**
rubber (material)	**guma** f
rubber (eraser)	**guma** f
rubber band	**gumička** f
rubbish	**smetí** n
Rubbish!	**Hloupost!**
rucksack	**ruksak** m
rude	**neomalený**
ruins	**trosky**
ruler (measuring)	**pravítko** n
to run	**běžet**
rush-hour	**dopravní špička** f
rusty	**rezavý**

S

sad	**smutný**
safe (adj.)	**bezpečný**
safe (container)	**sejf**
safety pin	**spínací špendlík** m
sail	**plachta** f
sailing (sport)	**plachtění** n
sailing boat	**plachetnice** f
sailor	**námořník** m
saint	**svatý/svatá**
sale	**výprodej** m
sales representative	**obchodní zástupce/ zástupkyně**
salmon	**losos** m
salt	**sůl** f
salty	**slaný**
same	**stejný**
sample	**vzorek** m
sand	**písek** m
sandals	**sandály**
sandwich (open)	**obložený chléb** m
sanitary towels	**vložky**
sauce	**omáčka** f
saucepan	**rendlík** m
saucer	**podšálek** m
to save (rescue)	**zachránit**
to save (money)	**ušetřit**
to say	**říct**
How do you say ...?	**Jak se řekne ... ?**
People say that	**Říká se, že ...**
That is to say ...	**Jinými slovy ...**
scales (weighing)	**váhy**
scarf	**šátek** m/**šál** m
scene (theatre)	**scéna** f
scene (view)	**krajina** f
scenery	**scenérie** f
scent	**vůně** f
school	**škola** f
science	**věda** f
natural science	**přírodní vědy** pl
scientist	**vědec/vědkyně**

scissors	**nůžky**
score: what's the score?	**jaké je skóre**
scratch	**rýha** f
scratch (on skin)	**škrábnutí** n
screen (cinema)	**filmové plátno** n
screen (TV, etc.)	**obrazovka** f
screw	**šroub** m
screwdriver	**šroubovák** m
sculpture	**socha** f
sea	**moře** n
season (of year)	**roční období** n
season ticket	**časová jízdenka** f
seat (place at a table, etc.)	**místo** n
seat (car, etc.)	**sedadlo** n
seat-belt	**bezpečnostní pás** m
second	**druhý**
second (time)	**vteřina** f
second-hand	**použitý**
secret	**tajemství** n
secret	**tajný**
secretary	**sekretářka** (male form unusual)
section	**úsek** m
to see	**vidět**
I can't see	**Nevidím**
I see	**Chápu/Aha**
to seem	**zdát se**
It seems ...	**Zdá se, že ...**
self-catering	**bez stravování**
self-service	**samoobsluha** f
to sell	**prodávat**
semi-skimmed milk	**polotučné mléko** n
to send	**poslat**
senior citizen	**starší občan**
sensible	**rozumný**
sentence	**věta** f
sentence (prison)	**rozsudek** m
separate	**oddělený**
serious	**vážný**
serious (important)	**závažný**
to serve	**obsluhovat**
service (hotel, etc.)	**obsluha** f
service (church)	**bohoslužba** f
services	**služby**
several	**několik**
to sew	**šít**
sewing	**šití** n
sex (gender)	**pohlaví** n
sex (intercourse)	**pohlavní styk** m
shade (colour)	**odstín** m
shadow	**stín** m
shampoo	**šampon** m
shampoo and blow-dry	**umýt a vyfoukat**
sharp	**ostrý**
to shave	**oholit**
shaving cream/ foam	**holicí krém** m/ **pěna** f
she	**ona**

sheep	**ovce** f
sheet (bed)	**prostěradlo** n
shelf	**police** f
shell (egg, nut)	**skořápka** f
shelter	**přístřeší** n
shiny	**lesklý**
ship	**loď** f
shirt	**košile** f
shock (electrical)	**elektrický šok** m
shock (emotional)	**šok** m
shoes	**boty**
shoelace	**tkanička** f
shoe polish	**krém** m **na boty**
shoe shop	**obchod** m **s obuví**
shop	**obchod** m
shop assistant	**prodavač/ prodavačka**
shopping: to go shopping	**jít nakupovat**
shopping area	**obchodní čtvrť** f
shopping centre	**nákupní středisko** n
short	**krátký**
shorts	**šortky**
to shout	**křičet**
show	**představení** n
to show	**ukázat**
shower	**sprcha** f
to shrink	**srazit se**
shut	**zavřený**
to shut	**zavřít**
shutter (window)	**okenice** f

shutter (camera)	**závěrka** f
sick (ill)	**nemocný**
to be sick	**zvracet**
to feel sick	**cítit se špatně**
side	**strana** f
sieve	**síto** n
sight (vision)	**zrak** m
sights (tourist)	**turistické atrakce**
sightseeing	**turistická prohlídka** f
sign	**nápis** m
to sign (one's name)	**podepsat**
signature	**podpis** m
silent	**tichý**
silk	**hedvábí** n
silver	**stříbro** n
similar (to)	**podobný**
simple	**jednoduchý**
since	**od (té doby co...)**
Since yesterday	**Od včerejška**
Since I came ...	**Od té doby, co jsem přijel** (male)/ **přijela** (female)
to sing	**zpívat**
single (room)	**jednolůžkový pokoj** f
single (ticket)	**na jednu cestu**
single (unmarried)	**svobodný**
sink	**dřez** m
sir	**pane**

sister	**sestra**	slippers	**pantofle**
sister-in-law	**švagrová**	slippery	**kluzký**
to sit	**sedět**	slow	**pomalý**
Sit down!	**Posaďte se!** (formal)	slowly	**pomalu**
		small	**malý**
size (shoes)	**velikost** f	to smell: it smells bad	**páchne to**
skates (on ice)	**brusle**		
to skate	**bruslit**	It smells good	**Voní to**
skis	**lyže**	smile	**úsměv** m
to ski	**lyžovat**	to smile	**usmívat se**
ski boots	**lyžařské boty/ přezkáče**	smoke	**kouř** m
		to smoke	**kouřit**
skiing	**lyžování**	smoked	**uzený**
ski lift	**lyžařská lanovka** f	smooth	**hladký**
skin (face)	**pleť** f	snake	**had** m
skin (body)	**kůže** f	to sneeze	**kýchat**
skin-diving	**sportovní potápění** n	snow	**sníh** m
		to snow: it's snowing	**sněží**
ski pole	**lyžařská hůl** f	so (thus)	**tak**
skirt	**sukně** f	soap	**mýdlo** n
ski run	**sjezdovka** f	sober	**střízlivý**
sky	**obloha** f	social worker	**sociální pracovník/ pracovnice**
to sleep	**spát**		
sleeper (on train)	**spací vagón** m		
sleeve	**rukáv** m	socks	**ponožky**
slice (cake)	**řez** m	socket (electrical)	**zásuvka** f
slice (ham, etc.)	**plátek** m	soda (water)	**sodovka** f
sliced	**plátkový/ krájený**	soft	**měkký**
slide film	**film** m **na diapozitivy**	soft drinks	**nealkoholické nápoje**
slim	**štíhlý**		
slip	**kombiné** n	soldier	**voják** m

181

sold out	**vyprodaný**	spanner	**klíč** *m* **na matice**
It's sold out	**Je vyprodáno**	spare (replacement)	**náhradní**
so many/so much	**tolik**		
some	**nějaký, trochu**	spare (left over)	**přebývající**
some milk	**trochu mléka**	spare time	**volný čas**
some bananas	**nějaké banány**	spare wheel	**rezerva** *f*/ **náhradní kolo** *n*
I'll have some	**Dám si trochu**		
somehow	**nějak**	sparkling (wine)	**šumivý**
someone	**někdo**	to speak	**mluvit**
something	**něco**	special	**speciální**
sometimes	**někdy**	speciality	**specialita** *f*
somewhere	**někde**	spectacles	**brýle**
son	**syn**	speed	**rychlost** *f*
song	**píseň** *f*	speed limit	**omezená rychlost** *f*
son-in-law	**zeť**		
soon	**brzy**	to spend (money)	**utrácet**
as soon as possible	**co nejdříve**	to spend (time)	**trávit**
		spice	**koření** *n*
sore: I have a sore throat	**Bolí mě v krku**	spicy	**kořeněný**
		spinach	**špenát** *m*
sorry (pardon me)	**promiňte**	spirits (alcohol)	**lihoviny**
I'm sorry	**Je mi líto**	splinter	**tříska** *f*
sort (type)	**druh** *m*	to spoil	**zkazit**
sound	**zvuk** *m*	sponge	**houba** *f*
soup	**polévka** *f*	sponge (cake)	**piškot** *m*
sour	**kyselý**	spoon	**lžíce** *f*
south	**jih** *m*	teaspoon	**čajová lžička** *f*
southern	**jižní**	spot (place)	**místo** *n*
souvenir	**suvenýr** *m*	on the spot	**na místě**
space	**prostor** *m*	sprain	**výron** *m*
spade	**rýč** *m*	spray	**sprej** *m*
		spring (season)	**jaro** *n*

square (town)	**náměstí** n	stepdaughter etc.	**nevlastní dcera**
square (shape)	**čtverec** m	sterling: pound	**libra** f **šterlinků/**
stadium	**stadion** m	sterling	**anglická libra** f
stain	**skvrna** f	stick	**hůl** f
stainless steel	**nerez** m	to stick	**přilepit**
stairs	**schody**	sticking plaster	**náplast** f
stalls (theatre)	**křesla**	sticky	**lepivý**
stamp (postage)	**známka** f	still	**(stále) ještě**
to stand	**stát**	still (non-fizzy)	**nešumivý**
stapler	**sešívačka** f	sting	**bodnutí** n
star	**hvězda** f	to sting (insect)	**bodat**
start (beginning)	**začátek** m	stock exchange	**burza** f
to start	**začínat**	stockings	**punčochy**
starter (food)	**předkrm** m	stolen: my ... has	**ukradli mi ...**
state (nation)	**stát** m	been stolen	
station	**nádraží** n	stomach	**žaludek** m
station master	**náčelník stanice**	stomach-ache	**bolení** n **žaludku**
stationer's	**papírnictví** n	stomach upset	**podrážděný**
statue	**socha** f		**žaludek** m
stay	**pobyt** m	stone (mineral)	**kámen** m
to stay (live)	**bydlet**	stop (bus)	**zastávka** f
to stay (remain)	**zůstat**	to stop	**zastavit**
steak	**biftek** m	Stop!	**Zastavte!**
to steal	**ukrást**	stopcock	**uzavírací kohout**
steam	**pára** f		m
steel	**ocel** f	storey	**podlaží** n
steep	**strmý**	story	**příběh** m
step (footstep)	**krok** m	stove	**sporák** m
step (stair)	**schod** m	straight	**přímý**
step-	**nevlastní**	straight on	**rovně**
stepchildren	**nevlastní děti**	strange (alien)	**cizí**
		strange (odd)	**divný**

strap	**řemínek** m	sunburn: suffer from sunburn	**spálit se na slunci**
straw (drinking)	**brčko** n	sunglasses	**sluneční brýle**
strawberries	**jahody**	sunshade	**sluneční** m
stream	**potok** m	sunstroke	**úpal** m
street	**ulice** f	suntan cream	**opalovací krém** m
street light	**pouliční osvětlení** n	supermarket	**supermarket** m/ **velkoprodejna** f **potravin**
stretcher	**nosítka** pl	supper	**večeře** f
strike (work)	**stávka** f	suppose: I suppose so/not	**předpokládám, že ano/ne**
string	**provázek** m		
stripe	**pruh** m	suppository	**čípek** m
striped	**pruhovaný**	sure	**jistý**
strong	**silný**	Sure!	**Jistě!**
to study	**studovat**	surface	**povrch** m
stupid	**hloupý**	surname	**příjmení** n
style	**styl** m	surprise	**překvapení** n
styling mousse	**pěnové tužidlo** n	surprised	**překvapený**
subtitled	**s titulky**	surrounded (by)	**obklopený**
suburbs	**předměstí** n sg	to sweat	**potit se**
success	**úspěch** m	sweater	**svetr** m
successful	**úspěšný**	sweatshirt	**mikina** f
such	**takový**	sweet	**sladký**
suddenly	**náhle**	sweetener	**sladidlo** n
suede	**semiš** m	sweets	**sladkosti**
sugar	**cukr** m	swelling	**oteklina** f
sugar lump	**kostka** f **cukru**	to swim	**plavat**
suit (clothes)	**oblek** m	swimming	**plavání** n
suitcase	**kufr** m	swimming pool	**plavecký bazén** m
summer	**léto** n	swimming trunks	**plavky** pl
sun	**slunce** n	swim suit	**plavky** pl
to sunbathe	**opalovat se**		

switch	**vypínač** m
to switch off (light)	**zhasnout**
to switch off (engine)	**vypnout**
to switch on (light)	**rozsvítit**
to switch on (engine)	**zapnout**
How do you switch it on?	**Jak se to zapíná?**
swollen	**oteklý**

T

table	**stůl** m
tablet	**tableta** f
table tennis	**stolní tenis** m
tailor	**krejčí**
to take	**vzít**
to take (bus, etc.)	**jet**
to take to	**zavézt**
to take off (clothes)	**svléknout se**
to take time	**trvat**
taken (seat)	**obsazený**
talcum powder	**zásyp** m
tampon	**tampón** m
to talk	**hovořit/mluvit**
tall	**vysoký**
tame	**krotký**
tap (water)	**kohoutek** m
tape	**páska** f
tape measure	**pásmo** n

tape measure (sewing)	**krejčovský metr** m
tape recorder	**magnetofon** m
taste	**chuť** f
tasty	**chutný**
tax	**daň** f
taxi rank	**stanoviště** n **taxíků**
tea	**čaj** m
tea bags	**pytlíkový čaj** n
to teach	**učit**
teacher	**učitel/učitelka**
team	**tým** m
teapot	**čajová konvice** f
to tear	**trhat**
teaspoon	**čajová lžička** f
teat (for baby bottle)	**dudlík** m
tea-towel	**utěrka** f
technical	**technický**
teenager	**teenager**
telephone directory	**telefonní seznam** m
to telephone	**telefonovat**
television	**televize** f
to tell	**říct**
temperature	**teplota** f
to have a temperature	**mít teplotu**
temporary	**dočasný**
tender (meat)	**křehký**
tennis	**tenis** m

tennis court	**tenisový kurt** *m*
tennis shoes	**tenisky/adidasky**
tent	**stan** *m*
tent peg	**kolík** *m*
terrace	**terasa** *f*
terrible	**strašný**
thank you (very much)	**děkuji pěkně/ mockrát děkuji**
that (that one)	**tamten**
That's why	**proto**
theatre	**divadlo** *n*
their/theirs	**jejich**
them	**je/jim**
for them	**pro ně**
with them	**s nimi**
then (at that time)	**tehdy**
then (later on)	**pak**
there	**tam**
therefore	**proto**
there is/there are	**je/jsou**
they	**oni**
thick (fat)	**tlustý**
thief	**zloděj/zlodějka**
thin (things)	**tenký**
thin (people)	**štíhlý**
thing	**věc** *f*
to think	**myslet**
I think so/not	**myslím, že ano/ myslím, že ne**
thirsty	**žíznivý**
I'm thirsty	**mám žízeň**

this (one)	**tento** *m*, **tato** *f*, **toto** *n*
thread	**vlákno** *n*
throat	**krk**
through	**skrz**
to throw	**hodit**
to throw away	**zahodit**
thumb	**palec** *m*
thunder	**hřmění** *n*
ticket (to travel)	**jízdenka** *f*
ticket (theatre, etc.)	**lístek** *m* **vstupenka** *f*
ticket office	**pokladna** *f*
tidy	**uklizený**
tie	**vázanka** *f*
tight (clothes)	**těsný**
tights	**punčocháče**
till (until)	**dokud**
time	**čas** *m*
What time?	**V kolik hodin?**
There's no time	**Není čas**
times	**-krát**
three times/four times, etc.	**třikrát/čtyřikrát**
timetable	**jízdní řád** *m*
tin	**konzerva** *f*
tinfoil	**alobal** *m*
tinned	**konzervovaný**
tin-opener	**otvírák** *m* **na konzervy**
tip (money)	**spropitné** *n*
tired	**unavený**

tissues	**papírové kapesníky**
to	**do, k**
toast (cheers)	**přípitek** m
toast (bread)	**topinka** f
tobacco	**tabák** m
tobacconist's	**tabák** m
today	**dnes**
together	**spolu**
toilet	**záchod** m
toilet paper	**toaletní papír** m
toiletries	**toaletní potřeby**
toilet water	**toaletní voda** f
toll	**poplatek** m
tomato	**rajče** n
tomorrow	**zítra**
tongue	**jazyk** m
tonight	**dnes večer**
too (also)	**také**
too (excessively)	**příliš**
too many/much	**příliš mnoho**
tool	**nářadí** n
tooth	**zub** m
toothache: I have toothache	**bolí mě zub**
toothbrush	**kartáček** m **na zuby**
toothpaste	**pasta** f **na zuby**
toothpick	**párátko** n
top (of mountain)	**vrcholek** m
top floor	**nejvyšší patro** n
torch	**svítilna** f

torn	**roztržený**
total (money)	**celkem**
total (complete)	**úplný**
to touch	**dotknout se**
tough (meat)	**tuhý**
tour (excursion)	**prohlídka** f
tourism	**turismus** m
tourist	**turista/turistka**
tourist information office	**turistická informační kancelář** f
to tow	**odtáhnout**
towards	**směrem k**
towel	**ručník** m
tower	**věž** f
town	**město** n
town centre	**centrum** n
town hall	**radnice** f
towrope	**vlečné lano** n
toy	**hračka** f
track (path)	**stezka** f
tracksuit	**tepláková souprava** f
trade union	**odborový svaz** m
traffic	**dopravní provoz** m
traffic jam	**dopravní zácpa** f
traffic lights	**dopravní světla**
trailer	**přívěs** m
train	**vlak** m
by train	**vlakem**
trainers	**tenisky/adidasky**

tram	**tramvaj** f
tranquilliser	**uklidňující prostředek** m
to translate	**překládat**
translation	**překlad** m
translator	**překladatel/ překladatelka**
to travel	**cestovat**
travel agency	**cestovní kancelář** f
traveller's cheque	**cestovní šek** m
travel-sickness	**cestovní nevolnost** f
tray	**podnos** m
treatment	**ošetření** n
tree	**strom** m
trip	**cesta** f
trolley	**vozík** m
trousers	**kalhoty**
trout	**pstruh** m
true	**pravdivý**
It's true	**Je to pravda**
to try	**zkusit**
to try on	**zkusit si**
T-shirt	**tričko** n
tuna	**tuňák** m
tunnel	**tunel** m
to turn: turn right/ left	**zahnout doprava/doleva**
turning (side road)	**odbočka** f
to turn off	**odbočit**

to turn off (engine)	**vypnout**
to turn off (tap)	**zavřít**
twice	**dvakrát**
twins	**dvojčata**
twisted	**zkroucený**
type (sort)	**typ** m
to type	**psát na stroji**
typewriter	**psací stroj** m
typical	**typický**

U

ugly	**ošklivý**
ulcer	**žaludeční vřed** m
umbrella	**deštník** m
uncle	**strýc**
uncomfortable	**nepohodlný**
under	**pod**
underground	**metro** n
underneath	**dole**
underwear	**spodní prádlo** n
to understand	**rozumět**
unemployed	**nezaměstnaný**
unfortunately	**naneštěstí**
unhappy	**nešťastný**
uniform	**uniforma** f
unpleasant	**nepříjemný**
to unscrew	**odšroubovat**
unusual	**neobvyklý**
unwell: I'm unwell	**není mi dobře**
up (go up)	**nahoru**

up (be up)	**nahoře**
upper	**horní**
upstairs	**nahoře**
urgent	**naléhavý**
urine	**moč** f
us	**nás, nám, námi**
for us	**pro nás**
to us	**k nám**
with us	**s námi**
without us	**bez nás**
use	**použití** n
to use	**používat**
useful	**užitečný**
useless	**k ničemu**
usual	**obvyklý**
as usual	**jako obvykle**
usually	**obvykle**

V

vacant	**volný**
vacuum cleaner	**vysavač** m
vacuum flask	**termoska** f
valid	**platný**
valley	**údolí** n
valuable	**cenný**
valuables	**cennosti**
van	**dodávka** f
vanilla	**vanilka** f
vase	**váza** f
VAT	**DPH** f
veal	**telecí** n

vegetable	**zelenina** f
vegetarian (noun)	**vegetarián/ vegetariánka**
vegetarian (adj.)	**vegetariánský**
vehicle	**vozidlo** n
vermouth	**vermut** m
very/very much	**velmi**
vest	**nátělník** m
vet	**veterinář/ veterinářka**
via	**přes**
video cassette	**videokazeta** f
video recorder	**video** n
view	**pohled** m
in my view	**podle mého názoru**
villa	**vila** f
village	**vesnice** f
vinegar	**ocet** m
vineyard	**vinice** f
virgin	**panna** f
Virgin Mary	**Panna Marie**
visit	**návštěva** f
to visit (places, people)	**navštívit**
visitor	**návštěvník/ návštěvnice**
voice	**hlas** m
volleyball	**volejbal** m
voltage	**napětí** n
to vote	**volit**

wage	**mzda** f
waist	**pas** m
waistcoat	**vesta** f
to wait (for)	**čekat (na)**
waiter/waitress	**číšník/číšnice**
waiting-room	**čekárna** f
walk	**procházka** f
to walk	**jít (pěšky)**
I'll walk	**půjdu pěšky**
Is it a long walk?	**Je to pěšky daleko?**
to go for a walk	**jít na procházku**
walking stick	**hůl** f
wall (house)	**stěna** f
wall (outside)	**zeď** f
wallet	**náprsní taška** f
walnut	**vlašský ořech** m
to want	**chtít**
war	**válka** f
warm	**teplý**
to wash	**mýt**
to wash (oneself)	**mýt se**
washbasin	**umyvadlo** n
washing (clothes)	**prádlo** n
washing powder	**prací prášek** m
to wash up	**mýt nádobí**
washing-up liquid	**prostředek** m **na mytí nádobí**
wasp	**vosa** f

wastepaper basket	**koš** m **na papír**
watch (wristwatch)	**hodinky** pl.
to watch (TV, etc.)	**dívat se (na)**
watchstrap	**řemínek** m **na hodinky**
water	**voda** f
waterfall	**vodopád** m
waterproof	**nepromokavý**
water resistant	**vodotěsný**
water-skiing	**vodní lyžování** n
wax	**vosk** m
way (route)	**cesta** f
this way	**tudy**
way in	**vchod** m
way out	**východ** m
way (method)	**způsob** m
we	**my**
weather	**počasí** n
What's the weather like?	**Jaké je počasí?**
wedding	**svatba** f
week	**týden** m
weekday	**všední den** m
weekend	**víkend** m
weekly	**týdně**
to weigh	**vážit**
weight	**váha** f
welcome	**přivítání** n
to welcome	**přivítat**
well (water)	**studna** f

well (adv.)	**dobře**	to win	**vyhrát**
I'm well	**Mám se dobře**	Who won?	**Kdo vyhrál?**
well done (steak)	**dobře propečený**	wind	**vítr** *m*
West	**západ** *m*	windmill	**větrný mlýn**
Western	**západní**	window	**okno** *n*
wet	**mokrý**	shop window	**výloha** *f*
what	**co**	windy	**větrný**
What is it?	**Co je to?**	It's windy	**Je větrno**
wheel	**kolo** *n*	wing	**křídlo** *n*
wheelchair	**invalidní vozík** *m*	winter	**zima** *f*
when	**kdy**	with	**s**
where	**kde**	without	**bez**
where is/are ...?	**kde je/jsou ... ?**	woman	**žena**
which	**který**	wonderful	**nádherný**
while (moment)	**chvilka** *f*	wood (trees)	**les** *m*
while (during)	**zatímco**	wood (material)	**dřevo** *n*
white	**bílý**	wool	**vlna** *f*
who	**kdo**	word	**slovo** *n*
Who is it?	**Kdo je to?**	work	**práce** *f*
whole	**celý**	to work	**pracovat**
wholemeal bread	**celozrnný chléb** *m*	world (adj.)	**svět** *m*
whose	**čí**	world (of the world)	**světový**
why?	**proč?**	First/Second World War	**první/druhá světová válka** *f*
why not?	**proč ne?**	worry	**starost** *f*
wide	**široký**	to worry	**dělat si starosti**
widow	**vdova**	Don't worry	**Nedělej si starosti**
widower	**vdovec**		
wife	**manželka**	worse	**horší**
wild	**divoký**	worst	**nejhorší**
win	**výhra** *f*		

worth: it's worth (... ing)	**stojí to za ...**
It's not worth it	**Nestojí to za to**
to wrap	**zabalit**
to write	**psát**
writing paper	**psací papír** m
wrong	**špatný**
You're wrong	**Mýlíte se** (formal)/ **Mýlíš se** (informal)
What's wrong?	**Co se děje?**
There's something wrong (with)	**Něco není v pořádku (s)**
Sorry, wrong number	**Promiňte, to je omyl**

X

X-ray	**rentgen** m

Y

yacht	**jachta** m
to yawn	**zívat**
year	**rok** m

yellow	**žlutý**
yes	**ano**
yesterday	**včera**
yet	**už, ještě**
Has he come yet?	**Už přišel?**
Not yet	**Ještě ne**
you (informal sg)	**ty**
you (formal sg)	**vy**
you (pl)	**vy**
young	**mladý**
your (informal sg)	**tvůj**
your (formal sg)	**váš**
your (pl)	**váš**
youth	**mládí** n
youth hostel	**mládežnická ubytovna** f

Z

zero	**nula** f
zip	**zip** m
zoo	**zoo** n/ **zoologická zahrada** f